ADVENTURES Around CINCINNATI

A Parent's Guide to Unique and Memorable Places to Explore with your Kids

ADVENTURES
Around
CINCINNATI

A Parent's Guide to Unique and Memorable Places to Explore with your Kids

LAURA HOEVENER and TERRI WEEKS

Hourglass Press
Milford, OH

Hourglass Press
Milford, OH
www.hourglasspress.net

Disclaimer: All recreational activities include a certain amount of risk. The publisher and authors disclaim any responsibility and any liability for any injury, harm, or illness that may occur through or by use of any information in this book.

Although every attempt was made to ensure the information contained in this book was accurate at time of printing, prices, hours, and availability of any of the destinations listed may change at any given time. The publisher and authors assume no responsibility for errors or inaccuracies. Any slights against any entries or organizations are unintentional.

Trademarked names, including names of destinations, are used in this book in an editorial context with no intention of infringement of the trademark.

All Scripture quotations in this publication are from the Contemporary English Version Copyright © 1991, 1992, 1995 by American Bible Society, used by Permission.

ISBN-10 - 0615482775
ISBN-13 - 9780615482774
LCCN – 2011906550

Cover Design by Alan Pranke
Typeset by Melanie Shellito

To buy books in quantity or schedule a speaking engagement, contact the authors.

Email: contactus@adventuresaroundcincinnati.com
Website: www.adventuresaroundcincinnati.com
Facebook: Adventures Around Cincinnati
Twitter: AdventureCincy

Printed in the United States of America

ACKNOWLEDGMENTS

Laura would like to thank:

My wonderful husband, John, for providing advice and being supportive of my many hours working on this project; my children, Daniel, Anna, and Morgan, for being willing and cheerful adventurers; Terri for being a great friend, co-author, and committed adventure partner; my friends and family for supporting me and praying for me on this book writing adventure; and my mom for always being there for me. I couldn't have written this book without the support and encouragement from all of you!

Terri would like to thank:

My amazing husband, Curtis, for taking this project seriously and spending many hours reading and critiquing; my children, Connor, Corinne, and Camille, for your enthusiasm about our adventures and this book; Laura, for your friendship, your Adventure Tuesday partnership, and for getting us started on the speaking and writing journey; and my parents, family, and friends who have encouraged me along the way. You are all precious to me.

Both of us would like to thank:

Paula Goodnight of Where's My Pen? Copywriting and Editing Services, for your many hours of work on this project and all your helpful advice; Ann Albin, for your many hours of work drawing and revising our maps; Nina Roesner of Greater Impact Ministries for mentoring us along our book-writing journey; to Connie Hammer, for the photography; Sharon Siepel, for all your support and encouragement; and Joni Sullivan Baker of Buoyancy Public Relations, for your guidance and help. A million thanks to our readers and fans for your suggestions, your enthusiasm and your dedication to adventures —it has meant more than you will ever know. Lastly, we thank God, our provider, for the inspiration to write this book and His help along the way.

TABLE OF CONTENTS

Part One
CREATING MEMORIES WITH YOUR FAMILY

Part Two
ATTRACTION LISTINGS

Part Three
PLANNING HELP

INTRODUCTION

As a parent, grandparent, caregiver, or anyone involved in the lives of children, you want to make the most of the days you spend with them. Wouldn't it be satisfying to plan a summer or a year full of new and different activities your children will enjoy? Do you want to create traditions they recall with fondness someday? This book encourages you to be intentional about having fun and creating memories while exploring your surroundings with your kids. It supplies a wide variety of suggested attractions, while also providing practical planning tips.

We are moms, and we know what it is like to have kids at home. Moms and dads need to cook meals, wash laundry, scrub bathrooms, and entertain kids. Even with all the work involved, it is important to carve out some recreational time to spend with your kids. If you schedule this time and are proactive about making plans, you are rewarded with some precious experiences that are imprinted forever in the minds of you and your children.

We started writing this book after six years of planning weekly summer "adventures," as we call them, with our kids. Since its inception, our adventures have brought us many priceless moments with our children and gave us the chance to see new experiences through their eyes. These weekly excursions are a part of our identity and have created a tradition that our kids won't let us bring to an end! We found some amusing, unique, and educational locations, each one adding another page to the scrapbook of our children's lives. With each adventure, we explore the area around us, learn something new, and enjoy each other's company. Many attractions are open year round, and if you can fit them into your schedule, you won't regret it. We have planned adventures over spring break, on weekends, and on school holidays. Summer break, though, has been our best opportunity for weekly plans and squeezing all we can out of the kids' school vacation.

Of course, there are other ways to use this book. We realize not everyone is a stay-at-home parent nor has summers off. You could also plan monthly adventures on weekends that include your spouse, or use this book to arrange a "staycation" (stay-at-home vacation). Another option is to find something refreshing to do with out-of-town guests or plan a lively weekend trip with your family. Homeschooling families may plan field trips fitting in with their current area of study.

Parents don't have a lot of time to read a long book, so we've made this concise and easy-to-follow. Do you want to have adventures with the kids in your life? If your answer is yes, then read on as we explain exactly how we make this tradition with our kids so special.

What is an Adventure?

We define an adventure as a planned outing on a day we set aside to explore a new destination with our kids. That day on our calendar is considered off-limits for scheduling other activities. An adventure location might be scenic, entertaining, or educational. We generally keep the cost low, too. Any new and interesting site becomes the setting of another adventure. Kids are happy doing simple things, like climbing the steps up and down the Serpentine Wall at Sawyer Point. They also enjoy structured activities such as attending a field trip with several friends at the airport. We found that planning activities is one of the keys to success. Without a plan, it's easy to let great ideas become forgotten and undone. This book helps you be intentional about making the most of the time that you have together.

When you take a vacation, do you study the travel brochures and try to squeeze in as many activities as possible? When you're away from home, it seems there are so many interesting things to see and places to go. Well, with an "adventures" mindset, you end up finding fascinating places right in your own backyard. When you become a hometown tourist, you'll be amazed at all the entertaining destinations waiting to be discovered.

In Part One of this book, we share our experiences and give advice on how to plan and execute your own adventures.

Part Two is a listing of kid-tested attractions within a two-hour drive from Cincinnati. In order to make it user-friendly for parents, we've included features like age recommendations and stroller-friendliness, so you can plan adventures suited to your own family's needs.

Part Three organizes the attractions into different categories to help you plan. Do you want to visit a museum? Look it up on our easy-to-use Attraction Table. Do your kids love animals? It's on the table, too. We hope this table will help you quickly find an outing that matches your interests. We've also included sample itineraries for summer and year-round adventures, for readers who want to get a quick start with limited planning.

Part One

CREATING MEMORIES
WITH YOUR FAMILY

WHY ADVENTURES?

The Birth of Summer Adventures

It was the summer of 2003 and we had scheduled an outing with some friends at Parky's Farm at Winton Woods Park. We had recently invited a speaker to our MOPS (Mothers of Preschoolers) group to talk about the many fascinating destinations in the state of Ohio. We were both avid sightseers when living in other states, but had been unfamiliar with much of what Cincinnati had to offer. We were inspired to visit the many attractions, but overwhelmed with figuring out how to make it a reality. While at the park, we talked about trying to get together on a regular basis with our kids to explore our city as tourists would. We realized we would have to be deliberate about it. We picked a day that worked each week for both of us, made a commitment to each other to keep that day available, and our Summer Adventures were born!

That first summer was full of joy, learning, and some challenges, too. Our babies weren't even a year old yet. Besides the babies, together we had three other children under the age of five. We were still dealing with diapers, naptimes, nursing, sippy cups, and an occasional temper tantrum. It certainly wasn't always easy, but it was unforgettable. As our kids have gotten older, our adventures have evolved. We can now travel farther, plan longer days, and even be riskier in our choices. What we've learned is that outings can be tailored to children of any age and to any kind of family. Even infants can travel along. Our daughters, Anna and Camille, think it's neat they've been going on adventures for as long as they can remember.

Our Kids Love Adventures!

We started weekly summer adventures in 2003 and haven't stopped yet because our kids love them! As soon as the weather starts warming up in the spring, they start asking about the upcoming summer's adventures. When we first started speaking to different groups and venues about our adventures, we asked our kids for their thoughts regarding our summer adventures. We heard some very positive answers. They like the excitement of new experiences. Terri's oldest daughter Corinne thinks it's cool to have opportunities like petting a shark at the Newport Aquarium. They like to remember past adventures and talk about their favorites. They like to explore new places and spend time with their friends. Terri's son Connor said that it makes history interesting and fun.

Each year, Laura's son Daniel requests to go blueberry picking. He has great memories of this, and each year, per his request, we do it again. Was this our favorite? Well, here's the story: It was the summer of 2003, our first year of adventures. Blueberry picking sounded like a great family activity. We envisioned children happily picking berries, a nice picnic lunch, and perhaps working together to bake a yummy pie or cobbler for dessert. The day was uncomfortably hot and sticky. As we walked with our berry buckets in hand, our two oldest boys (ages three and four at the time) were challenging each other to a berry picking competition. This battle never slowed down.

"I have the most berries of the kids!"

"No, I have the most berries!"

"NO, I do!"

"NO, I DO!"

This seemed to go on and on...and on and on. Now

remember, it was REALLY hot and muggy. On the bright side, there were plump, ripe berries everywhere, and we all felt compelled to keep picking. Pretty soon my (Laura's) baby started to fuss and nursing was the only thing that was going to make her happy. With nowhere to sit down, I stood in front of a blueberry bush, holding a nursing baby with one hand and picking blueberries with the other. I wasn't about to let those kids pick more blueberries than I did! All in all, it was a hot, sticky, miserable day, but we keep doing it again and again each year. Each year it's always my son's favorite adventure. To top things off we take home some delicious berries to enjoy.

HOW CAN ADVENTURES BENEFIT YOUR FAMILY?

Memories for a Lifetime

There are so many benefits that come from adventures it is hard to know where to begin. The most long-lasting benefit is the priceless memories you create that are cherished for the rest of your lives. Make sure to take your camera along to document your adventures. Half of the fun is reliving them with your kids when you look back at the pictures. If you like to scrapbook, get ready for some extra work. All of your new excursions will provide plenty of material for some terrific scrapbook pages!

A Tradition to Remember

We've been planning adventures for so long our kids assume these will always be a part of their summer plans. In fact, our crew doesn't remember a summer without them. They look forward to seeing their friends each week and experiencing something out of the ordinary. It has become a part of who we are as a family. Having a tradition like this makes your kids feel like they are a part of something special. As the parents and planners, we look forward to scheduling our summers and anticipating the experiences we will have. After eight years, we still have a list of places we haven't yet visited and plan on continuing our adventures into and through our kids' teen years. We are having too much fun to let adventures end.

A Family that Plays Together, Stays Together

In his book, *Keep the Siblings, Lose the Rivalry*, Dr. Todd Cartmell says, "The amount of positive family bonding time you spend together with your children will have a direct impact on the quality of their relationships (with each other) when you're not around." So, if kids are having fun with each other, they will actually get along better the rest of the time. Being intentional about planning recreational time together really helps your kids interact more positively with each other! It can also be gratifying to give your family shared experiences to remember together.

Prepare Kids for Challenges

When we look at the values that we want to instill in our kids, we can see how these adventures are shaping them. According to Licensed Professional Clinical Counselor Bill Ramsey, exposing children to different experiences and hands-on learning opportunities stimulates their brains in an important way. Their experiences form the foundation of their belief systems that determine how they deal with challenges for the rest of their lives. Exposure to a wide range of experiences helps them to think broadly and opens their minds to more possibilities.

Expand your Comfort Zone

We found that planning different adventures each week requires us to get out of our comfort zones. Going to the pool every week or choosing a favorite park to visit would be easier than constantly finding new activities. Our hope as parents is that our children will develop a view that new experiences are exciting rather than scary. If they are at ease with the idea of leaving their comfort zones, then they will be better equipped as adults to face the unknown.

The Confidence Builder

Taking our kids on adventures has given us the experience and confidence to plan longer adventures and family vacations that allow us to see other parts of the country and world. A few years ago we attempted our first overnight adventure. A low-cost airline was offering a deal we couldn't pass up, so we flew to Kansas City for an overnight trip. Late-night flights made it challenging, but it was a trip that none of us will forget. A few years ago, Terri's family made a goal to visit all 50 states. They also took a month-long trip to Scandinavia. While there, Terri even took her kids to two countries on her own after her husband returned to the US. This might have been very unnerving without the confidence gained through our adventures. What might have seemed impossible a few years ago starts looking more feasible as you gain more experience.

Bill Ramsey also attests that adventures build kids' confidence, especially if you are able to return to some of your favorite places. The first time they visit a place, they explore it. The second time they begin to take control and organize ideas. If you continue to return to a favorite spot, eventually the kids start feeling like experts. Although we advocate seeing new places, there are some solid reasons to make repeated visits to favorite locations, especially if your kids request it. On that note, while we generally try to plan new adventures, we do sometimes repeat one. We have decided sometimes we all enjoy a destination so much it's worth experiencing again. Others we have revisited because the younger kids were too young to remember or because the older ones will now be able to see it with more mature eyes.

Adding Structure

From a practical standpoint, having a weekly routine that includes adventures and other regular activities provides some needed structure in kids' summer schedules. Kids manage their emotions better when they know what to expect. My (Terri's) kids know that we do laundry on Monday, go on an adventure on Tuesday, go to the library on Wednesday, and go shopping and run errands on Thursday.

Knowing that adventures happen on Tuesday is also good for my (Laura's) family. We start the week off looking forward to Tuesday, and then the rest of the week can be spent doing whatever else needs to be done. The structure helps me to plan the tasks I need to accomplish during the week knowing that one day is unavailable. If I didn't have a planned day for an adventure, it might never happen. Something more urgent might take priority and we'd probably put off our adventure until the next week. Some structure can be a very good thing!

Take Some Risks, Reap the Rewards

When we plan our summers, we always put a few sure-fire winners into the schedule, but also take a risk or two and add some unknowns into the mix. For example, when we took a tour of the Verdin Bell and Clock Museum, we weren't sure how it would go over with the kids. But we knew that even if the kids hated it, we could assure them something better was planned for the next week. We can also stop at the park or treat the kids to ice cream afterwards to end a not-so-fun adventure on a positive note. Since we know we can fit about nine adventures into a summer, we can afford to take a few risks. We have had some rewarding and interesting experiences by taking these risks!

Accountability Makes All the Difference

We both knew we wanted to explore our region and be intentional about having fun and making memories with our kids. We also both knew we'd be more disciplined if we could commit to doing this with a friend. Accountability makes all the difference. If you make plans with someone who is expecting you to be there, it's a hard commitment to break. For instance, it would be easy to put off your own plans because you don't feel like packing a lunch, it might rain, or there is too much laundry to do. Knowing someone is counting on you helps you put the laundry off until the next day.

One summer, there was one week we both were extremely busy. There was no reason we should have tried to fit an adventure into our crazy schedules. Between the two of us, we had kids in swim lessons and in day camp, there were out-of-town visitors, a nephew being born, a camping trip to pack for and a vacation that was about to begin. We each knew the other person was counting on us, so we went ahead with our plans. It may not have been the smartest thing we've ever done, but it proves that with advanced planning and accountability, you can make anything happen.

That's What Friends are For

Through our adventures together, we have deepened our friendship over the years. In addition to the shared memories, we have had many conversations. We usually ride in one minivan and chat while we're driving. One of the most common responses we've heard after speaking to a group is, "I wish I had a friend like that." We want to encourage you that you can build a friendship like this and it's one of the many benefits of adventures. Occasionally we wish our husbands could join us, but we know spending time with a girlfriend is also healthy for our marriages. You can certainly attempt adventures by yourself, but they will be more enjoyable and memorable for the both the parent and the kids when you experience them with friends.

Sharing your Knowledge and Experience

Another benefit of adventures is when you have out-of-town visitors, you can take them somewhere unique. They will think you are an expert on your hometown! Most out-of-town visitors will have heard of Kings Island. We love Kings Island, too, but we can help our visitors stretch their money further by telling them of many other options. Some of the kids' grandparents have joined us for an adventure. Terri's mother-in-law drove all the way from Wisconsin because she said they sounded like so much fun she wanted to experience one herself. An adventure lifestyle is contagious! It makes us smile to think when our kids have their own families they will be able to pass down to their kids their memories of going on exciting adventures. Hopefully, someday we will be the grandmothers tagging along on our children's adventures with our grandchildren.

Mission Accomplished

We have found that at the end of the summer, we can look back with a great sense of accomplishment. Sure, there are always activities we didn't complete, but when we take an inventory of the new and interesting places we have been, we don't have any regrets about how we spent our days. It's a great feeling to know you've made every effort to make it memorable. We look forward to planning our next summer almost as soon as the last adventure has ended.

PLANNING AND EXECUTING YOUR OWN ADVENTURES

So you've decided that it would be a great idea to start adding adventures into your routine. What are the next steps? We've put together some ideas to help you make this a reality. We have included numerous planning tips to think about before you head out on your first adventure. This chapter contains all these ideas and tips together with our recommendations to achieve success.

How Will you Fit Adventures into your Life?

To begin, you will need to decide how you are going to incorporate adventures into your family's life. Depending on when you have available time, you could plan weekday or weekend adventures. Weekend adventures might make it easier to involve your spouse or the whole family. If you are at home during the weekdays, you could pair up with a friend, like we do, and explore during the day.

With whom will you go on your adventures? Will it be your spouse, a friend, or just you and the kids? If you're going to find a friend to share your adventures, you will need to decide who that will be. Look for someone with whom you get along well or someone you would like to know better and who has kids approximately the same ages as yours. You may want to try one or two adventures before committing to a whole summer. If you want to plan weekly excursions, you'll need a partner who is willing to make this kind of commitment. That's not to say there can't be exceptions to a weekly schedule. We usually average about nine adventures each summer, skipping a couple of weeks for vacations and camps.

As we shared in the last chapter, having an adventure partner has many benefits. The Bible has some good advice for us in this area:

You are better off to have a friend than to be all alone, because then you will get more enjoyment out of what you earn. If you fall, your friend can help you up. But if you fall without having a friend nearby, you are really in trouble.

Ecclesiastes 4:9-10 (Contemporary English Version)

Neither of us has ever literally fallen down during an adventure, but a partner can be there to help with many kinds of issues. A friend might help with reading a map, taking kids to the bathroom, or running to the car to fetch the first aid kit if someone scrapes a knee. We also share the joy of going through the experience together. A partner simply makes the time more enjoyable.

Can a group of friends plan adventures? Sure they can. From time to time, another friend will join us on an adventure. While this can be fun, it can also add complexity. With just two of us and our own children, we have increased flexibility and can more easily come to agreement on last minute changes. For example, there have been many times we delayed an adventure by an hour because the kids slept late. Other times we had planned on bringing lunches but changed our minds at the last minute because we didn't have anything convenient to pack. Additionally, if your group can all fit into a single vehicle, traveling can be more straightforward than with a caravan. We think that some of these smaller group benefits have been one of the reasons we've been successful.

Pick a Day

When are you going to have your adventures? We almost always have our adventure on Tuesdays. If you are doing weekend adventures, maybe you will always plan them on the second Saturday of the month. It might sound restrictive to do it the same day every week or month, but it's really easier than having a varied schedule. We generally don't make any other commitments on Tuesdays. On occasion, we've come across attractions we want to see that are closed on Tuesdays and we will switch to a different day that week. We can be as flexible as we need to be, but it works well for both of us to have a standing date.

Plan your Adventures

The next step is to decide which outings have the most appeal and then design an itinerary. We have found that it works best to plan a schedule that is adjustable enough to allow for changes. During our first summer we didn't make our plans in advance. Each week we decided our next activity, sometimes as late as the night before. The next year, we sat down together in April and filled in our calendars. We found that it was much less stressful to decide everything in advance. We recommend making a schedule and sticking with it unless something arises that requires a change.

If you are planning summer adventures, it's best to save any indoor adventures for the end of the season. The temperature tends to get hotter towards the end of July and August and sometimes it's just too miserable to enjoy being outside. If we have an unusually hot or a rainy day early in the summer, we select something else from our plan that is indoors, with shelter and air conditioning, and move the outdoor excursion to a later date. This also helps minimize the time spent indoors when the weather is beautiful. This strategy provides the freedom to change plans while still keeping you on track to include all your planned adventures for the summer.

If you are scheduling year round adventures, plan your outdoor adventures during the warmer months, but have a back-up activity in case the weather requires you to alter your plans.

Balance Activity Types

We have listed over 80 different attractions in this book. In the final section we have sorted the attractions into numerous categories such as museums, parks, animals, and historical sites. When we plan our summer, we try to select one or two destinations from each category. This broadens our experiences and keeps our outings refreshing for all of us. For example, one week we'll go to a botanical garden, the next week a factory tour, next a museum, and then a new park. Over the course of a summer you can learn some history, be entertained, get some exercise, reflect on art, and stimulate your minds in other ways. By scheduling a mix of adventures, you'll find that if one week isn't a big hit, there will be something new and different to look forward to the next time. We also have a category for free attractions to help you meet your budget goals. An occasional splurge can be justified when we balance it with several free or low-cost outings.

Logistically Speaking

This book's data was accurate at the time of printing, but keep in mind that operating hours and admission fees can change. Be sure to check the operating schedules before visiting. Decide in advance who will drive and who will be in charge of directions or a map. Having a GPS unit certainly reduces the reliance on directions and maps. Not only does it route you to your destination, but it provides an estimated arrival time. A GPS can also be used to find nearby restaurants and parks.

Don't Forget to Call

We have learned the principle "call ahead" the hard way. Websites are not always accurate, books may be out of date, and newspaper articles may have conflicting information. Once, we had heard about a restaurant where you eat ice cream while watching sky divers jump out of planes. They laughed when we called because this information had been out of date for ten years! We were relieved we didn't make that drive without checking our information first. A phone call is always your best option.

As another example, there was an historical village we had wanted to visit for years. According to their website, they were closed on our normal adventure day, so we changed plans to visit on a different day. When we arrived, there were no guides working that day, all the buildings were locked, and it was raining. While we weren't charged to get in, we found ourselves walking through an historical village in the rain and looking at the outsides of buildings. If we had called ahead, we would have learned they were experiencing a temporary shortage of tour guides and could have made plans to visit another time.

Diffuse Disappointments

As hard as you work at making plans, sometimes adventures don't turn out like you had hoped. But do not despair; they can still be redeemed! For instance, look for a nearby park and explore a playground. It's always prudent to pair any adventure that might be risky, meaning the kids might not like it, with something you know they will enjoy. To continue the story of our rainy and disappointing visit to the historical village, afterwards we went to Build-a-Bear Workshop at the mall and the kids had a great time. To avoid the need to improvise, you can be prepared for an alternate activity. When we planned our trip to Clifton Mill, an old-fashioned grist mill about an hour away, we weren't sure if the kids would enjoy the tour. In case this occurred, we also planned to dine at the adjoining restaurant that serves pancakes made from the freshly ground grain which we were positive the kids would love.

It is our recommendation to try some activities that you are uncertain the kids will enjoy. Sometimes our kids really surprise us by showing an interest in something that we wouldn't have anticipated. The Dayton Aviation Heritage National Historical Park has a small theater showing a documentary film about the Wright Brothers. We thought it might not appeal to young kids, but opted to see it anyway. Surprisingly, when the film ended, Terri's youngest daughter Camille, who was four at the time, declared that it was the best movie she'd ever seen and wanted to watch it again at home for movie night.

What's for Lunch?

If your adventure will last more than half a day, you'll need to consider plans for lunch. We've tried several different options for lunches, but to save money we usually pack our own meal. One year we took turns packing lunches to give each other a break. However, sometimes it makes sense to eat in a restaurant as part of the adventure. Our kids loved eating at Clifton Mill after taking a tour of the grist mill where they grind the wheat for the pancakes. Another restaurant adventure is Sky Galley, where you can eat while watching planes take off and land at Lunken Airport. There are some weeks when we have so much going on that we give ourselves permission to eat out so that we can take one task off our to-do lists.

Turn an Adventure into an Education

If you are interested in carrying the theme of the adventure through the week, you can supplement your outing with related books or activities.

Check out fiction and non-fiction books from the library that help you learn more about the subject. Or, rent a movie that enhances the experience. You could add other related activities, like crafts or games. We recommend starting with the adventures, and adding other activities as time and energy permit, after you are in a comfortable routine.

Opportunities Abound

This book is filled with a diverse collection of recommended attractions to begin your adventure planning. It includes all of our personal favorites compiled after our years of travels. We are constantly on the lookout for new ideas and encourage you to do the same. Remember to use local newspapers as a resource. In the summer and fall, they publish lists of U-pick farms for blueberries, strawberries, and apples. In addition, they itemize unique events, festivals, concerts, or plays around town. If you hear of something a friend has done, ask about it and write it down. If your kids like hiking, look into letterboxing (www.letterboxing.org) or geocaching (www.geocaching.com), which combine hiking with a mission of finding a hidden treasure. Be sure to look at the travel brochures while staying at a hotel. Stop at a visitor's center in your hometown or visit one in another city while traveling. Parks in your area or even a fast food or mall play area can also be great kid-pleasers. There are probably many entertaining destinations located near your neighborhood like bowling alleys, miniature golf, or go-carts. While these types of adventures will almost always be a hit with your kids, try also to look beyond typical attractions. Especially when you are in another city, search for something unique to the area. Unique locations may end up being more memorable for your family than seeing the latest movie release. Keep your eyes and ears open and you are sure to find a memorable adventure!

On your Mark, Get Set, Go!

In the following pages, you'll find many years' worth of our own adventures. We wanted to be sure that all of our listings were "tested" by our kids, so at least one of our families has personally visited and approved all of them. Now, your next step is to follow our guidelines and start a new adventure tradition with your kids. You will be encouraged by the excitement you see in your kids. Pick something you are sure your kids will like and create a new memory!

We know there are still an abundance of places to see and activities to do that aren't included in this edition. As we explore new places, we plan to list them on our website, Facebook page, and tweet about them on Twitter. If you have a suggestion for a listing to include on our website or in a future edition of this book, please let us know, and we will be sure to check it out. We love hearing from people who have heard us speak and then planned their own adventures. Please contact us and share your experiences. We wish you many priceless memories with your family as you start your own tradition of adventures!

Email: contactus@adventuresaroundcincinnati.com
Website: www.adventuresaroundcincinnati.com
Facebook: Adventures Around Cincinnati
Twitter: AdventureCincy

Part Two

ATTRACTION LISTINGS

CENTRAL CINCINNATI AND NEWPORT, KENTUCKY

ATTRACTIONS

1. BB Riverboats
2. Carew Tower Observation Deck
3. Cincinnati Art Museum
4. Cincinnati Fire Museum
5. Cincinnati History Museum at Cincinnati Museum Center
6. Cincinnati Reds Hall of Fame & Museum
7. Cincinnati Zoo & Botanical Garden
8. Duke Energy Children's Museum at Cincinnati Museum Center
9. Fountain Square
10. Krohn Conservatory
11. Lunken Airport Playfield
12. Museum of Natural History and Science at Cincinnati Museum Center
13. National Underground Railroad Freedom Center
14. Newport Aquarium
15. Purple People Bridge
16. Ride the Ducks - Newport
17. Robert D. Lindner Family OMNIMAX Theater at Cincinnati Museum Center
18. Sawyer Point and Serpentine Wall
19. Sky Galley Restaurant at Lunken Airport
20. UnMuseum at the Contemporary Arts Center
21. Verdin Bell and Clock Museum
22. William Howard Taft National Historic Site
23. World Peace Bell

Note that attractions 5, 8, 12, and 17 are in the same location.

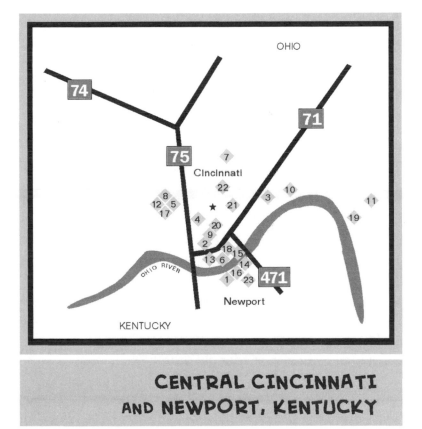

OHIO

74

71

75

7

Cincinnati

22

8
12 5
17

4

20

9

2

3 10

21

11

19

18
15
13 6

14

16
1 23

471

Newport

OHIO RIVER

KENTUCKY

CENTRAL CINCINNATI
AND NEWPORT, KENTUCKY

BB RIVERBOATS

Address: 101 Riverboat Row, Newport, KY 41071

Phone: (859) 261-8500
(800) 261-8586

Website: www.bbriverboats.com

Hours: Daily sightseeing cruises, Memorial Day through Labor Day

90 minute sightseeing cruises; see website for departure times.

Boarding time is 20 min. prior to cruise time.

Dining, holiday and special cruises also available; check website for details.

Cost: $15.00 Adults
$9.00 Children (4–12)
Free Children 3 and under, but ticket required
$13.50 Seniors

Check for discounts in the Entertainment Book.

Ages: All ages

Stroller and wheelchair friendly: Yes

Length of visit: 2 hours (allow extra time for boarding)

Description and comments:

Enjoy a view of Cincinnati and Northern Kentucky's landmarks from the river. Go up to the open air top deck for the best views or sit in air-conditioned comfort on a lower deck. The captain broadcasts a commentary during the 90-minute cruise, pointing out landmarks and sharing some history. Older children may take an interest in the commentary, but it's best to bring some toys or coloring books to occupy younger children if they start to get restless. Since riverboats are an important part of Cincinnati's history, we think everyone should take a riverboat cruise at least once. A snack bar and restrooms are available. Each child receives a free ice cream sandwich on either the Harbor Cruise or the Ice Cream Social Cruise.

Consider booking the Friday afternoon "Pirates of the Ohio Cruise" for even more fun for kids. Little pirates receive a pirate hat, eye patch, and treasure map and play pirate games during the cruise.

CAREW TOWER OBSERVATION DECK

Address: 441 Vine Street, Cincinnati, OH 45202
             Corner of Fifth and Vine across from
             Fountain Square

Phone: (513) 579-9735 Observation Deck
             (513) 241-3888 to arrange for group discounts

Hours: Monday–Friday: 10 a.m.–6 p.m.
             Saturday and Sunday: 10 a.m.–7 p.m.

Cost: $2 Adults
             $1 Children (6–11)
             Free Children 5 and under
             Call ahead for group discounts

Ages: All ages

Stroller and wheelchair friendly: No

Length of visit: 1 hour plus time to eat or shop
                  at Tower Place Mall

Description and comments:

For many years, Carew Tower was the tallest building in Cincinnati. Now it is the second tallest. It rises 49 stories and 574 feet over downtown Cincinnati near the Ohio River. To visit the observation deck, ride the elevator to the 45th floor. At this point, you'll need to leave your stroller behind. Next, board a tiny elevator and ride to the 48th floor, then climb the steel stairway to your destination. On a clear day, visitors can see for miles into Ohio, Kentucky and Indiana. The observation deck is appropriate for all ages, but be aware that smaller kids will need a boost to see over the wall. This can be challenging if you have several kids who all need to be held in order to see the view. The wall is approximately 42" tall. Kids taller than about 54" will be able to see easily over the fence without help. The wind is sometimes strong, so be prepared with a jacket or sweater. Also, be sure to stop at the restrooms on the ground level as there are no facilities on the observation deck.

Carew Tower is a must-see attraction in Cincinnati. The building itself is a National Historic Landmark, and the view is spectacular. While visiting, notice the Art Deco design of the building. One interesting fact is that construction began on Carew Tower in September 1929, one month before the stock market crashed. The work continued, but only the first three floors were built with the impressive details. After this, plain brick was used on the remaining floors.

After you're finished admiring the city from above, do some downtown shopping or grab a bite to eat in the Tower Place Mall food court, located on the basement level.

Parking is available in the Tower Place Mall parking garage. Street parking is also available.

CINCINNATI ART MUSEUM

<u>Address:</u>　953 Eden Park Drive, Cincinnati, OH　45202

<u>Phone:</u>　(513) 639-2995　General
(513) 639-2971　Education Center
(877) 472-4226

<u>Website:</u>　www.cincinnatiartmuseum.org

<u>Hours:</u>　Tuesday–Sunday:　11 a.m.–5 p.m.
Closed some holidays

Artworld:
Saturday and Sunday:　11 a.m.–5 p.m.

<u>Cost:</u>　Museum admission is free
$4 Parking

<u>Ages:</u>　2 and up (when Artworld is open)

<u>Stroller and wheelchair friendly:</u>　Yes

<u>Length of visit:</u>　1–4 hours

<u>Description and comments:</u>

Your visit to the Cincinnati Art Museum should definitely include a stop at Artworld, located on the ground floor. Designed especially for kids, Artworld is an education center where kids can create their own masterpiece and engage in several hands-on activities. Even toddlers will find this area interesting. The area has a theme which changes several times a year. Artworld is open only on weekends from 11 a.m.–5 p.m.

The galleries appeal to older children. Stop by the front desk to receive a Family Guide and a map. The Family Guide, which changes monthly, often includes a scavenger hunt.

This gives the kids a mission as they explore the galleries. Upon completion of the scavenger hunt, return it to the front desk to receive a prize. Another way we have found to keep the kids' interest is to ask them to pick out their favorite piece in each gallery and tell us why they like it.

Most of the museum is decidedly hands-off (they might scold kids even for standing too close to the art), but there are a few places that have hands-on exhibits, including galleries 137 and 141 in the Asian art section. The museum has paintings from well-known artists such as Picasso, Van Gogh, Monet, Manet, Pissarro, Renoir, and Cezanne. It also has other forms of art such as sculpture, pottery, woodcarving, and metalwork, and includes art from many time periods and parts of the world. If you choose to take younger children into the galleries, we recommend keeping them in a stroller.

The Cincinnati Art Museum has many programs for children and families. Some programs are free and some require a fee. These run from September through May. Free programs include Family ARTventures (Saturdays at 1 p.m. and Sundays at 3 p.m.), Family First Saturday (first Saturday of the month, 1–4 p.m.), and Wee Wednesdays (last Wednesday of the month, 10–11:30 a.m.). Check the website for information on other programs.

CINCINNATI FIRE MUSEUM

Address: 315 W. Court Street, Cincinnati, OH 45202

Phone: (513) 621-5553

Website: www.cincyfiremuseum.com

Hours: Tuesday–Friday: 10 a.m.–4 p.m.
         Saturday and Sunday: Noon–4 p.m.
         Closed holidays

Cost: $7 Adults
        $5 Children (7–17)
        Free Children 6 and under, with adult or
        senior admission
        $6 Seniors (65+)

        Parking is in metered spots on street. Bring
        coins to feed meter.

        Check for discounts with AAA or
        Entertainment Book.

Ages: 2 and up

Stroller and wheelchair friendly: Yes

Length of visit: 1–2 hours

Description and comments:

A trip to the Cincinnati Fire Museum is both educational and entertaining. A favorite for young kids is the cab of a fire engine. Kids can climb into it, push buttons to turn on the lights, and pretend they are off to fight a fire. Everyone can slide down a fire pole to the lower level and watch a movie about fire safety. The history of firefighting in Cincinnati is explained starting from its earliest days with a bucket brigade. Kids like to pretend to pump water with an old style hand pumper. A safe house exhibit teaches about fire safety in the home. Try out the interactive computer exhibits. Older kids may show an interest in the exhibits on antique fire engines and equipment.

CINCINNATI HISTORY MUSEUM AT CINCINNATI MUSEUM CENTER

Address: 1301 Western Avenue, Cincinnati, OH 45203

Phone: (513) 287-7000

Website: www.cincymuseum.org

Hours: Monday–Saturday: 10 a.m.–5 p.m.
Sunday: 11 a.m.–6 p.m.

Cost: $8.50 Adults
$6.50 Children (3–12)
$4.50 Children (1–2)
Free Children under 1 with adult
$7.50 Seniors (60+)

$6 Parking

Discounts are offered if you visit more than one museum or see an OMNIMAX film. Check website for more information. Check for discounts in the Entertainment Book.

An annual family membership to all three museums (Duke Energy Children's Museum, Museum of Natural History and Science, and Cincinnati History Museum) with free parking and free or discounted admission to 200+ museums worldwide is $130. We highly recommend this option.

Ages: 3 and up

Stroller and wheelchair friendly: Yes

Length of visit: 2–4 hours

Description and comments:

The Cincinnati History Museum opens a window into Cincinnati's past. Upon entering the museum, you find yourself immersed in a model of Cincinnati with each neighborhood set in a different decade. The model includes working trains, inclines, and moving vehicles. Learn about the history of each neighborhood at interactive computer stations. Each month the museum creates an "I Spy" challenge for kids in which they must locate objects that have been hidden in the model. Check at the information desk to find out the challenge of the month. Behind the model, there are train tables to keep the little ones occupied. The trains must be checked out at the information desk. There is no charge, but they will keep your ID until you return the trains.

Next you pass through the Cincinnati Goes to War exhibit, where you climb aboard a streetcar and listen to a commentary. Wander past other displays and push the buttons to hear stories about people's lives during that time. Continuing through the museum, you find exhibits on Cincinnati's settlers, including Native Americans, pioneers, and immigrants. Watch an interactive video on the earthworks built by Native Americans. Visit a log cabin where there are often demonstrations such as carding wool or sewing. Kids learn about Ohio's transportation history by maneuvering a canal boat through a canal with locks at a wooden model built especially for kids. Then climb aboard a model of a flatboat, the moving van of the frontier. Learn about how pioneers built these boats, then disassembled them at their destination and used the wood to build their houses. Kids try this themselves at a kid-sized version of a boat and house with removable boards.

On the lower level, you'll feel like you've stepped into another time at Cincinnati's Public Landing. Step aboard a recreated steamboat and learn what makes the paddle wheel turn. Visit a working print shop and see how documents were printed before computers were invented. Peek in the windows of various shops and interact with costumed interpreters. Finally, visit the recreated 1910 machine shop with working machinery.

Frequent Museum Center visitors should look into "employment" for kids ages 6 and up at the C.U.T. (Cincinnati Union Terminal) House Detective Agency. When new detectives are "hired," they will be issued a case file, notebook, and pencil, and are sent out to solve mysteries. They must visit different parts of the museum to solve the mysteries and then report back to the Chief Inspector with their findings. They earn money (in special C.U.T. currency) for each mystery they solve and can spend it on merchandise in the detective store. Detectives are recognized with promotions to higher ranks in the organization as they solve more mysteries. There is a one-time fee of $5 to participate in this fun program. Check the Calendar of Events on the website to find out about the many free scheduled activities in the museum.

CINCINNATI REDS HALL OF FAME & MUSEUM

Address: 100 Main Street, Cincinnati, OH 45202

Phone: (513) 765-7923

Website: http://reds.mlb.com/cin/hof/index.jsp

Hours: November–March
             Tuesday–Sunday: 10 a.m.–5 p.m.

             April–October (Non-game days)
             Daily: 10 a.m.–5 p.m.

             April–October (Game days)
             Saturday and Sunday: 10 a.m.–two hours after
             end of game for afternoon games
             Saturday and Sunday: 10 a.m.–8 p.m. for all
             evening games

Cost: $10 Adults
             $8 Children (5–17)
             Free Children 4 and under, active military
             and veterans
             $8 Seniors (60+)

Ages: 3 and up

Stroller and wheelchair friendly: Yes

Length of visit: 2 hours

Description and comments:

If you have a baseball fan in your family, be sure to visit
the Cincinnati Reds Hall of Fame & Museum. Here you
learn the history of the Reds, the oldest franchise in Major
League Baseball, and about the 78 (at printing time) Hall
of Famers showcased in the museum. Start your visit by

sitting in the grandstand and watching a 12-minute movie about Pete Rose. You'll see a number of Pete Rose displays including a view of the exact spot his record-breaking 4,192nd hit landed. You'll also see a rose garden with a white rose bush commemorating the exact location of this hit.

Visit the Red's Front Office where you'll notice historic documents and discover the history behind famous trades and decisions made by the staff. The traditional gallery contains oodles of baseball memorabilia. Visitors may also try their hand at fielding, batting, and pitching. Feel a 95-mph fast ball zoom past you, stand on the mound and attempt pitching a ball into the strike zone, then leap into the air to snag that important catch. Kids under 6 have their own play space including small lockers complete with a dress up area containing Reds jerseys.

Pick up the microphone and jump into a broadcast by Marty Brennaman and Joe Nuxhall and call a close play for them. Next, listen to Marty and Joe call the same play. Relax on the "front porch" and listen to Waite Hoyt and Joe Nuxhall recall memories from their careers.

The Ultimate Reds Room is decorated like a home rec room including a vast collection of bobbleheads, pennants, signs, and baseball cards. You can watch a show with bloopers and highlights while sitting in seats from Riverfront stadium.

Relive the glory days of the Big Red Machine and walk among figures of eight life-sized famous players. Scores of items are dedicated to explaining the history of baseball through the years, including the 1919, 1940, and most recently 1990 World Series Championships.

Finally, enter the Hall of Fame, where each Hall of Famer is commemorated with a plaque. Look for your favorite player and learn more about the history of our Cincinnati Reds.

Tours of Great American Ball Park are available upon request. Call in advance to schedule.

CINCINNATI ZOO & BOTANICAL GARDEN

<u>Address:</u>   3400 Vine Street, Cincinnati, OH 45220

<u>Phone:</u>   (513) 281-4700

<u>Website:</u>   www.cincyzoo.org

<u>Hours:</u>   Daily
           January–May: 9 a.m.–5 p.m.
           May–September: 9 a.m.–6 p.m.
           September–December: call for hours

<u>Cost:</u> $14 Adults
           $10 Children (2–12)
           $10 Seniors (62+)
           $8 Parking

           Additional fees for rides and 4D theater.
           Package pricing available. Check for discounts
           with AAA, Kroger card, or Entertainment Book.

<u>Ages:</u>   All ages

<u>Stroller and wheelchair friendly:</u> Yes

<u>Length of visit:</u> 2–6 hours

<u>Description and comments:</u>

What can we say? Cincinnati has a great zoo! The Zagat Survey calls it the number one attraction in Cincinnati and one of the top zoos in the nation. *Child Magazine* has named it one of the "10 Best Zoos for Kids." Before you go, check the website for self-guided tours with attractions specially suited for kids or for ideas for a rainy or cold day.

You'll find many exhibits at the zoo for everyone to explore. It's amusing to visit Gibbon Island to watch these animals swinging and chasing each other on their natural playground. Stop by Giraffe Ridge and feed the giraffes crackers from the palm of your hand. Gorillas, manatees, polar bears, penguins, insects, eagles, and wolves are other favorite attractions. Visit Siegfried & Roy's famous white lions. Don't miss the petting area in the Children's Zoo, either.

Many inside attractions make the zoo fun for a cold or rainy day too. Manatee Springs, 4D Special FX Theatre, Nocturnal House and the Discovery Forest are just a few of the inside attractions that will keep you from being soaked if the weather turns bad.

Also, gaze at the stunning annuals, perennials, trees, plants and grasses that make up the Botanical Gardens. See the zoo website for more information on the different varieties of plants.

Train and tram rides are available (for an extra fee), along with a carousel ride.

DUKE ENERGY CHILDREN'S MUSEUM AT CINCINNATI MUSEUM CENTER

Address: 1301 Western Avenue, Cincinnati, OH 45203

Phone: (513) 287-7000
           (800) 733-2077

Website: www.cincymuseum.org

Hours: Monday–Saturday: 10 a.m.–5 p.m.
           Sunday: 11 a.m.–6 p.m.

Cost: $8.50 Adults
           $6.50 Children (3–12)
           $4.50 Children (1–2)
           Free Children under 1 with adult
           $7.50 Seniors (60+)

           $6 Parking

           Discounts are offered if you visit more than one
           museum or see an OMNIMAX film. Check
           website for more information. Check for
           discounts in the Entertainment Book.

           An annual family membership to all three
           museums (Duke Energy Children's Museum,
           Museum of Natural History and Science, and
           Cincinnati History Museum) with free parking
           and free or discounted admission to 200+
           museums worldwide is $130. We highly
           recommend this option.

Ages: 1–12

Stroller and wheelchair friendly: Yes

Length of visit: 2–5 hours

Description and comments:

The Duke Energy Children's Museum is one of three museums in the Cincinnati Museum Center complex at Union Terminal. It has consistently ranked in the top ten children's museums in the world. Little Sprouts Farm is a separate area for families with children age four and under. It includes an area with slides, play gardens, a sand table, a pretend row boat, story times, and puppet shows. It also contains a Parent Resource Area and a private area for nursing moms and babies. The entrance to Little Sprouts Farm is supervised to prevent little ones from leaving without you. Park your stroller in the "parking lot" outside the farm and prepare to spend hours with your preschoolers.

Kids (ages 3–7) pretend to be grown-ups in Kids Town, an area including a grocery store, diner, veterinary office, kitchen, and play house. Buying groceries, delivering mail, taking animal x-rays, and ordering and preparing meals to serve to customers at the diner are some of the activities for this age group.

In Energy Zone, the giant ball play area, the kids grab a bag and scurry to collect thousands of balls off of the floor. Use the blasting air jets to float a ball in mid air. Try to pedal an exercise bike to power a ball conveyor, launch a ball into a basket using air pressure, and be prepared for a giant shower of colorful balls when you hear the alarm bell ring.

Find three stories of climbing fun in The Woods. Your children will be thrilled to climb in the trees, whiz down the slide, cross rope bridges, search for fossils, and explore a small cave. The Woods houses a large aquarium filled with fish and turtles. Your children can search for the secret tunnel ending "inside" the water. This area is best for kids over age five who can navigate the sometimes challenging climbing areas.

You will want to visit the many other areas in the museum where you can try to assemble a large arch with foam shapes, construct a skyscraper using blocks, pound nails into buildings, visit children who live in other countries, splash in the water play area, load "rocks" into a crane, and dump them into a dump truck. Watch for special posted activities your children might enjoy, too.

The entrance to Union Terminal contains a Rotunda with a few lunch options. An abundance of tables are available, and you are permitted to carry in your lunch. While in the Rotunda, be sure to look at the ceiling to observe the two 20' x 105' mosaics depicting the history of Cincinnati. These mosaics were commissioned in 1932. Other mosaics are found near the entrance to the OMNIMAX Theatre. The Museum Center originally had many more of these murals decorating the building. During renovations, these murals have been moved to the Greater Cincinnati/Northern Kentucky International Airport.

The Children's Museum can be crowded in the mornings, with fewer visitors after lunch. If your children have outgrown naps, afternoon is your best bet. Remember to bring a change of clothes in case your kids get carried away in the water play area. You won't want to leave this fun-filled museum!

FOUNTAIN SQUARE

Address: 520 Vine Street, Cincinnati, OH 45202

Phone: (513) 979-4738

Website: www.myfountainsquare.com

Hours: Always open
Call for skating hours

Cost: Free to visit Fountain Square
$3 Admission for skating
$3 Skate rental

Ages: All ages

Stroller and wheelchair friendly: Yes

Length of visit: 30 minutes–2 hours

Description and comments:

Fountain Square is at the heart of downtown Cincinnati. It was recently redesigned with garden-like landscaping, a 24' x 42' video board and a refurbished fountain, The Genius of Water.

Uniformed Ambassadors are always present to keep Fountain Square clean and safe. Play chess or checkers on one of sixteen tables with preprinted boards. Obtain game pieces at the parking garage office on blue level one. They will hold your driver's license in exchange for the pieces.

Tyler Davidson Fountain is the focal point of Fountain Square. It was dedicated in 1871. The nine-foot-tall Genius of Water stands in the center of the fountain with other figures surrounding it showing the practical and recreational uses of water. Walk the perimeter of the fountain and notice the different animals and people on each side. The Water Wall is the other amusing feature at Fountain Square. A sheet of water pours down the wall and also spouts up from the ground. Kids might get a little wet running through and putting their hands in the water.

Surrounding Fountain Square are many shops and restaurants, including Graeter's famous ice cream. It is also fun to watch the horse drawn carriages circling the square.

KROHN CONSERVATORY

Address: 1501 Eden Park Drive, Cincinnati, OH 45202

Phone: (513) 421-4086

Website: http://www.cincinnatiparks.com/krohn-conservatory/index.shtml

Hours: Tuesday–Sunday: 10 a.m.–5 p.m.
Extended hours during special show
and events

Cost: Donations only, except during special events

Butterfly Show:
$6 Adults
$4 Children (5–16)
Free Children 4 and under
$5 Seniors
$20 Family Pack (2 Adults and up to 6 children)

Ages: All ages

Stroller and wheelchair friendly: Yes

Length of visit: 1–2 hours

Description and comments:

Located in Eden Park, Krohn Conservatory houses more than 3,500 plant species from all over the world. Walk into the Palm House and feel as though you have been transported into a rainforest, surrounded by palm trees and other tropical plants, and a waterfall. Next, visit the Desert House with its cacti and other succulents. The conservatory also has collections of bonsai, orchids, and a tropical house. One room is reserved for seasonal displays and events. Our favorite is the Butterfly Show, held each year from mid-April to mid-June. Bright flowers fill the room and butterflies flutter around, landing on flowers and sometimes on people. Kids will be delighted trying to hold one on their finger. Stop by the craft room where kids can make a simple craft. It is best to attend on a sunny day, when butterflies are the most active.

LUNKEN AIRPORT PLAYFIELD

Address: 4740 Playfield Lane, Cincinnati, OH 45226

Phone: (513) 321-7333

Hours: Land of Make Believe:
May–October
Daily: 9 a.m.–8:30 p.m.

Playground is free during off hours; use back gate for entrance. Restrooms not accessible during off hours.

Cost: $1 Children 12 and under (for the Land of Make Believe)
Free Adults

Ages: 1–9

Stroller and wheelchair friendly: Yes

Length of visit: 2–3 hours

Description and comments:

There are two playgrounds here to encourage kids to burn off some energy. The Land of Make Believe is fenced in so your little ones can't escape when you're not looking. Parents will be grateful for the shade that this park provides. It contains three large climbing structures and many other features including a sandbox to satisfy the younger kids. The $1 fee is truly worth it. The other playground is called the Spirit of '76 and is sunnier and not fenced in. There is no fee to play at this playground. You will find indoor air-conditioned bathrooms and a snack bar. The area also includes a golf course (regular and par 3), walking trails, tennis courts, and a baseball field. For lunch, either use the many picnic tables in the park or dine at the nearby Sky Galley restaurant (see separate listing).

MUSEUM OF NATURAL HISTORY AND SCIENCE AT CINCINNATI MUSEUM CENTER

<u>Address:</u>   1301 Western Avenue, Cincinnati, OH 45203

<u>Phone:</u>   (513) 287-7000

<u>Website:</u>   www.cincymuseum.org

<u>Hours:</u>   Monday–Saturday: 10 a.m.–5 p.m.
Sunday: 11 a.m.–6 p.m.

<u>Cost:</u> $8.50 Adults
$6.50 Children (3–12)
$4.50 Children (1–2)
Free Children under 1 with adult
$7.50 Seniors (60+)

$6 Parking

Discounts are offered if you visit more than one museum or see an OMNIMAX film. Check website for more information. Check for discounts in the Entertainment Book.

An annual family membership to all three museums (Duke Energy Children's Museum, Museum of Natural History and Science, and Cincinnati History Museum) with free parking and free or discounted admission to 200+ museums worldwide is $130. We highly recommend this option.

<u>Ages:</u>   2 and up

<u>Stroller and wheelchair friendly:</u> Yes

<u>Length of visit:</u> 2–4 hours

Description and comments:

The Museum of Natural History and Science is a wonderful place to take kids of all ages. The older they get, the deeper they delve into the exhibits. Upon entering the museum, stop at the Information Desk to pick up the monthly scavenger hunt. For each question they answer correctly, kids earn points to spend in the Nature's Trading Post. They can also bring in items like rocks and seeds to trade in for points. Check the website for guidelines.

Do not miss the All About You exhibit where kids engage in interactive activities that teach how various organs in the human body function. In Earth Stories, watch an interactive program about Native American earthworks and a film about the planets. See a replica of Neil Armstrong's spacesuit.

Kids love the cave exhibit, a reproduction of a limestone cave, complete with stalactites and stalagmites, a waterfall, and an underground stream. Explore one of the two paths through the cave, one that is suitable for strollers and wheelchairs, and a more adventurous route with stairs. Kids love to wiggle through tunnels and weave through different passageways. Look for the live bats and learn about other animals that live in caves.

Another favorite is the Ice Age exhibit. Examine pollen through a microscope and discover what you can learn about animals that lived long ago by inspecting their bones. Older kids use computers to create a virtual ice age animal and prevent an animal from becoming extinct. They can test their knowledge with questions on lift-up panels. Our kids gravitate to a water and sand table where they can witness how water from glaciers sculpts the landscape. Make sure you point out the cross-section of a California Redwood to your kids and explain how you can determine the age of the tree when it was cut down by counting the rings. This one was almost 1,400 years old! Trek through the ice cave and walk amongst models of animals of the ice age, including an elk, bison, mastodon, and sloth.

Finally, learn about fossils, extinction, and dinosaurs. Dinosaur-loving kids will be fascinated by the dinosaur models and skeletons. Take a closer look to see which bones are real and which were cast. Check out the dinosaur room with a play table, dinosaur film, and lots of books. The museum also has a variety of daily demonstrations and many free scheduled activities. Check the website and the Information Desk for more information.

NATIONAL UNDERGROUND RAILROAD FREEDOM CENTER

Address: 50 East Freedom Way, Cincinnati, OH 45202

Phone: (513) 333-7500
(877) 648-4838

Website: www.freedomcenter.org

Hours: Tuesday–Saturday: 11 a.m.–5 p.m.

Cost: $12 Adults
$10 Students (13–21)
$8 Children (6–12)
Free Children 5 and under, with paying adult
$10 Seniors

Check for AAA discount.

Ages: 8 and up

Stroller and wheelchair friendly: Yes

Length of visit: 2 hours

Description and comments:

The National Underground Railroad Freedom Center tells the important history of the underground resistance to slavery and the network of courageous people who risked their lives to help slaves escape. Learn how slaves were brought to the United States and how they were traded within the United States. One exhibit is an actual slave pen used by a Kentucky slave trader to hold slaves while moving them to slave markets. Go inside it and look for where the chains were attached. Most of the exhibits are beyond the understanding of younger children who may not understand the concept of slavery. The museum has created a complimentary audio tour designed for families and children. Your kids can identify the points on the tour and enter the corresponding number into the device and hold it up to their ear like a telephone to hear the commentary. They can listen to stories from the perspectives of both a young slave woman and a slave owner. The films are also a good choice for kids, especially "Brothers of the Borderland" because it helps them picture how the Underground Railroad operated.

NEWPORT AQUARIUM

Address: 1 Aquarium Way, Newport, KY 41071

Phone: (859) 261-7444

Website: www.newportaquarium.com

Hours: Daily: 10 a.m.–6 p.m.
Extended hours during summer and holiday seasons. Check website for details.

Cost: $22 Adults
$15 Children (2–12)
Free Children 1 and under

Annual passes are available for approximately the cost of two visits.

Ages: All ages

Stroller and wheelchair friendly: Strollers not permitted during summer months

Length of visit: 2 hours

Description and comments:

The Newport Aquarium has a variety of underwater exhibits that appeal to all ages. On any given visit, you might see a baby excitedly watching a turtle swim, a teenage couple on a date, or older couples without children. When you arrive, check the schedule to find out when there will be shows in the theater. You won't want to miss hearing scuba divers talk to you from inside the shark tank. There is much for the shark lover to experience. It is surreal to watch the sharks and shark rays swim right over your head as you walk through an acrylic tunnel. In Shark Central, you can pet a shark as it swims by you. Feel the thrill of being inside a shark cage in the Great White Shark Cage Dive. Don't worry — it's a film! At the end of your visit, you are routed through an open-air viewing area where you can see the shark tank from above.

Other exhibits show the diversity of aquatic habitats. Examples include a coral reef, mangrove forest, grass bed, and river environments. Kids love to look at the fish and compare and contrast their colors, shapes, sizes, reflectivity, and other characteristics. Linger in the jellyfish exhibit and become mesmerized watching the pulsing jellyfish. View alligators beneath you through a clear floor. Watch the playful otters and penguins. Informative videos are placed throughout the aquarium to help you learn more about the animals in the tanks. For a change of pace, stop by the Frog Bog where the kids climb and slide in the play area, play a video game, and learn from interactive exhibits. Visit the aviary where you can purchase nectar for $1 to feed the lorikeets. Kids are delighted to see the lorikeets up close, sometimes as close as sitting on your shoulder or head!

The admission cost for the Newport Aquarium is pricey, but the annual pass is reasonably priced at approximately the cost of two visits. Discounts or coupons can often be found on their website or in local newspapers. The aquarium also offers additional programs for a fee, such as behind-the-scenes tours and penguin encounters.

PURPLE PEOPLE BRIDGE

(official name is the Newport Southbank Bridge)

Address: Over the Ohio River between Pete Rose Way in Cincinnati and Third Street in Newport

Phone: (859) 655-7700

Website: www.purplepeoplebridge.com

Ages: All ages

Stroller and wheelchair friendly: Yes

Length of visit: 1 hour (allow time for other attractions)

Description and comments:

Yes, it's a purple bridge. Why purple? Because that's what color focus groups picked when it was restored. This pedestrian bridge was previously the L&N Railroad Bridge. It is the longest connector of its kind joining two states.

This pedestrian-only bridge is just over a half-mile long and takes you from Newport to Cincinnati with a carefree walk. Lanes are present for bikers, walkers and skaters. There are also park benches, handrails, security cameras, emergency call boxes, and trash cans on the bridge.

Combine a walk on the Purple People Bridge with a visit to Sawyer Point (see separate listing), Great American Ballpark or Paul Brown Stadium, dinner at a downtown restaurant, Newport on the Levee, or ice cream at Fountain Square. This bridge is a unique part of the Cincinnati/ Northern Kentucky area.

A private company used to offer a Purple People Bridge Climb. Visitors could climb the catwalk over the bridge. Please note that this is no longer offered as an attraction.

RIDE THE DUCKS – NEWPORT

<u>Address:</u>   1 Aquarium Way, Newport, KY 41071

<u>Phone:</u>   (859) 815-1439

<u>Website:</u>   www.newportducks.com

<u>Hours:</u>   Approximately mid-March through October or November, depending on weather

Typically four tours are scheduled on weekdays and 7–8 tours per day on weekends

Check website for details

<u>Cost:</u> $17 Adults
$12 Children (2–12)
Free Children 1 and under, but ticket required

<u>Ages:</u>   All

<u>Stroller and wheelchair friendly:</u> Wheelchairs are permitted. Strollers are not permitted on board, but can be stowed near the departure site.

<u>Length of visit:</u> 1 hour

<u>Description and comments:</u>

Perhaps you have seen these amphibious vehicle tours in other cities? Now the Cincinnati area also has Ride the Ducks. The vehicles are essentially a truck enclosed in a water-tight shell and were first used by the military in World War II. They drive on land, then drive into the water and operate as a boat. The 45-minute tour highlights landmarks in Cincinnati and Newport, with nuggets of history mixed in with the fun. Everyone on board is given a souvenir quacker and is encouraged to use it to quack at passers-by.

a duck boat tradition. The ducks depart from Newport on the Levee, cross a bridge into Cincinnati, and drive to Cincinnati Public Landing for the exciting splashdown into the Ohio River. On the river you'll see the waterfront areas of Cincinnati, Newport, and Covington, including a unique view of the Roebling Murals, painted on the flood walls of Covington. The tour continues on land through the streets of Cincinnati and Newport. This is a fun way to learn more about the history of the area!

Tickets can be purchased in advance on their website. We recommend calling to confirm tour times. The Coast Guard will not allow the tours to operate if the river level is too low or too high. Pick up your tickets at Newport on the Levee at a small building in front of the aquarium. The tours depart from Third Street, near Brio Restaurant.

ROBERT D. LINDNER FAMILY OMNIMAX THEATER AT CINCINNATI MUSEUM CENTER

Address: 1301 Western Avenue, Cincinnati, OH 45203

Phone: (513) 287-7000
(800) 733-2077

Website: www.cincymuseum.org

Hours: Monday–Saturday: 10 a.m.–5 p.m.
Sunday: 11 a.m.–6 p.m.

Cost: $7.50 Adults
$5.50 Children (3–12)
$6.50 Seniors (60+)

Discounts are offered if you visit a museum in addition to seeing an OMNIMAX film. Check website for more information.

Ages: 3 and up

Stroller and wheelchair friendly: Yes

Length of visit: 1 hour

Description and comments:

This OMNIMAX Theater is located at the Cincinnati Museum Center at Union Terminal. See high quality, family friendly documentaries on the recently renovated five-story, 72-foot diameter, tilted, domed screen. Pair this movie with one of the other museums for a discounted price. Be sure to check the website for available show titles and times. Tickets can be purchased online or at the Museum Center. Weekend shows sometimes sell out so it may be helpful to buy your tickets in advance. Please note that smaller children might be frightened by the intensity of the enormous screen and loud noises.

SAWYER POINT AND SERPENTINE WALL

Address: 801 E. Pete Rose Way, Cincinnati, OH 45202

Phone: (513) 352-6180

Website: www.sawyerpoint.com

Hours: 6 a.m.–11 p.m.

Cost: Free
           $2 Parking in Sawyer Point Lot

Ages: All ages

Stroller and wheelchair friendly: Yes

Length of visit: 2–4 hours

Description and comments:

Sawyer Point is a mile-long park along the banks of the Ohio River just south of downtown Cincinnati. The park has loads of things to do; this could be a whole day's adventure. Starting out, the kids will love 1,000 Hands playground, one of the best playgrounds in the area. Volunteers built this playground in just six days in 2003. It was specifically constructed so all kids could play together, including those in wheelchairs. The playground sits under the Big Mac Bridge (the yellow, arched bridge) so it provides lots of shade and protection from rain. The floor of the entire playground is covered with soft rubber flooring to keep the kids safe from injuries. Ramps and handicap accessible swings are also on hand. Zip lines, sandboxes, tire swings, towers, monkey bars, and slides add to the excitement, too.

Sawyer Point includes volleyball courts, tennis courts, and bike rentals. Several maps and signs throughout the park explain the history of Cincinnati and the river as a riverboat port, as part of the Miami-Erie Canal, and as a major industrial center. Stroll the River Walk and admire the statue of Cincinnati's namesake, Roman hero Lucius Quinctius Cincinnatus, welcoming you to Sawyer Point. The flood column on the statue marks the levels of the three great floods, including the 1937 flood that reached heights of almost 80 feet and devastated the surrounding area.

The Serpentine Wall is another favorite feature of Sawyer Point. The wall follows the river and has large curvy stair steps along the river bank. Climbing up and down the steps can keep kids happily entertained for quite a while. Watch the boats on the river and stroll down to Great American Ballpark, the home of the Cincinnati Reds. Admire the National Steamboat Monument at the Public Landing. It holds a 60-ton replica paddle wheel and steam is released every minute from the tall stacks.

Wander westward down the street and you'll find Concourse Fountain and Sprayground; a wet playground where the kids can cool off. This is located between the parking lots at Sawyer Point and the Public Landing. You'll have to walk to get there from either lot, so you might want to take a stroller. Remember to pack swimsuits, sunscreen, and towels for the kids.

SKY GALLEY RESTAURANT
AT LUNKEN AIRPORT

Address: 262 Wilmer Avenue, Cincinnati, Ohio 45226

Phone: (513) 871-7400

Website: www.skygalley.com

Hours: Sunday–Thursday: 11 a.m.–9 p.m.
Friday and Saturday: 11 a.m.–10 p.m.

Cost: $7–$8 sandwiches
$8–$10 salads
$11–$22 entrees
$4.95 Kids' menu

Ages: All ages

Stroller and wheelchair friendly: Yes

Length of visit: 1–2 hours

Description and comments:

The Sky Galley's big draw is its view – airplanes taking off and landing at Lunken Airport. The airport now serves private airplanes and corporate jets, but at its dedication in 1930 it was the largest municipal airport in the world. Sky Galley is located inside the airport terminal and, before it was converted into a restaurant, meals were prepared there for flights on American Airlines. You may dine indoors or out on the patio and the kids will be fascinated watching the planes. The prices are reasonable and there is a kids' menu with the typical choices (burgers, grilled cheese sandwiches, chicken tenders, etc.) available for $4.95 including beverage. Reservations are recommended, especially for large groups. Ask for a table with a good view of the planes.

UNMUSEUM AT THE
CONTEMPORARY ARTS CENTER

Address: 44 E. 6th Street, Cincinnati, OH 45202

Phone: (513) 345-8400

Website: www.contemporaryartscenter.org/unmuseum

Hours: Monday: 10 a.m.–9 p.m.
            (5–9 p.m. free admission)
            Tuesday: Closed
            Wednesday–Friday: 10 a.m.–6 p.m.
            Saturday and Sunday: 11 a.m.–6 p.m.

Cost: $7.50   Adults
            $4.50   Children (3–13)
            Free   Children 2 and under
            $6.50   Seniors (65+)
            Free admission on Mondays from 5–9 p.m.

            Check for AAA discount.

Ages: 3 and up

Stroller and wheelchair friendly: Yes

Length of visit: 1–2 hours

Description and comments:

    The UnMuseum at the Contemporary Arts Center is a
place to explore art in an out-of-the-box sort of way. The
entire 6th floor is filled with interactive exhibits for children.
Some of the exhibits are musical exhibits and most of the
exhibits are hands-on. In the Art Lab, which is stocked with
art supplies, kids can create their own masterpiece. The fee
includes admission to the entire center which has rotating

exhibits, but we suggest asking if any areas might not be appropriate for children.

There are special programs for families and children. The fourth Sunday of every month from 1–4 p.m. is Family Sunday. An artist or educator helps families create an art project. These projects are designed for ages 5 and up. Thursday Art Play is held on the second and fourth Thursday of each month from 1–2 p.m. This program is geared for younger children, ages 3–7, and a parent. Both programs are free with museum admission. On the first Saturday of each month is a program called "44." Although 44 is not designed specifically for children, some of the presentations are very appealing to them. This free program is held in the lobby and does not require museum admission. Check the website for details on this and other family-friendly programs.

VERDIN BELL AND CLOCK MUSEUM

Address: 444 Reading Road, Cincinnati, OH 45202

Phone: (513) 241-4010

Website: www.verdin.com/info/museum.asp

Hours: Guided tours are given by appointment only.

Cost: $3 per person

Ages: 8 and up

Stroller and wheelchair friendly: Yes

Length of visit: 1 hour

Description and comments:

The Verdin Company is a family company that has been producing bells and clocks since 1842, and the Verdin Museum displays historic bells and clocks that they have collected over the years. Verdin Company bells ring in many churches, bell towers, and institutions all over the world. The company headquarters and museum are situated in a restored 1850s church building. The building itself is striking and majestic with vaulted ceilings, stained glass windows, mosaics, and murals. Your tour guide will explain the history of the neighborhood, the church, the Verdin family, and the Verdin business. You also learn how the bells are manufactured. This tour is better suited for older children. The Verdin Company created the World Peace Bell which is also listed as an attraction in this book.

WILLIAM HOWARD TAFT
NATIONAL HISTORIC SITE

Address: 2038 Auburn Avenue, Cincinnati, OH 45219

Phone: (513) 684-3262

Website: www.nps.gov/wiho/index.htm

Hours: Daily: 8 a.m.–4 p.m.
Closed some holidays

Cost: Free

Ages: 8 and up

Stroller and wheelchair friendly: Wheelchair accessible
Strollers not allowed in the house

Length of visit: 1 hour

Description and comments:

Visit the William Howard Taft Home and Taft Education Center for a glimpse into what life was like in the early days of our 27th President of the United States and the 10th Chief Justice of the United States. Learn the history of how his family came to Cincinnati, and how he came to be the only person to have held the two highest positions in the United States of America. Guided tours are available every half hour. Begin your tour in the Taft Education Center and meet an animatronic figure of Charles P. Taft II, the son of William Howard Taft. Charles talks to visitors about his interesting family. There is also an orientation video which will explain more about the Tafts' lives.

The tour takes you through Taft's childhood home. Each room on the first floor is decorated in period pieces as it would have been at the time the Tafts occupied it. See the sitting room, the children's room, the library, and several other rooms. The upstairs rooms have been filled with displays about the life of his parents, siblings, and children. You'll also find a menu of a dinner served at a White House party.

The rangers are extremely knowledgeable and answer all your questions. This activity is probably best for children 8 and older, but younger children might appreciate seeing the house that a former president lived in as a child. For $1.50 you can purchase a Junior Ranger booklet which your child can fill out during and after the tour. Upon completion, they present it to a ranger, receive a certificate and pin, and are sworn in as a Junior Ranger.

WORLD PEACE BELL

Address: 425 York Street (4th & York),
Newport, KY 41071

Phone: (859) 581-2971

Website: www.verdin.com/info/world-peacebell.asp

Hours: Bell swings at five minutes before noon daily
Tours by appointment only

Cost: Free viewing of bell
Tour: $1 per person

Ages: All ages
Tours ages 5 and up

Stroller and wheelchair friendly: Yes

Length of visit: <1 hour

Description and comments:

The World Peace Bell is 12 feet tall and 12 feet wide and weighs 66,000 lbs. It is the world's largest free-swinging bell and first swung to ring in the year 2000. It swings daily at five minutes before noon. The bell was created by The Verdin Company and was cast in France. The bell is VERY loud, but kids can cover their ears and be entertained. You can stand directly underneath it and see the clapper strike the bell.

Group tours can be scheduled by appointment. The tour lasts approximately 45 minutes. During the tour you will go up to the bell bridge to see the bell at eye level. They will strike the bell so you can hear it and touch it to feel the vibration. You will learn about the history of the bell, who owns it, how it was made, the journey to get it there, and what the symbols at the top of the bell mean. Kids receive a copy of a poem and a drawing of the bell.

GREATER CINCINNATI

ATTRACTIONS

1. Adventure Station at Sharon Woods Park
2. Anderson Ferry
3. The Beach Waterpark
4. Behringer-Crawford Museum
5. Big Bone Lick State Park
6. Chilo Lock 34 Park
7. Cincinnati Nature Center - Rowe Woods
8. Cincinnati/Northern Kentucky International Airport
9. CoCo Key Water Resort
10. Coney Island
11. Creation Museum
12. Crooked Run Nature Preserve
13. EnterTRAINment Junction
14. Fort Ancient
15. Garden of Hope
16. Gorman Heritage Farm
17. Grant Boyhood Home
18. Grant Schoolhouse
19. Heritage Village Museum at Sharon Woods Park
20. Highfield Discovery Garden at Glenwood Gardens Park
21. Irons Fruit Farm
22. Jungle Jim's International Market
23. Kings Island and Boomerang Bay Waterpark
24. Lebanon Mason Monroe Railroad
25. Little Miami Bike Trail
26. Loveland Castle - Chateau LaRoche
27. Mariemont Bell Tower Carillon
28. Megaland at Colerain Park
29. Metamora, Indiana
30. Noah's Ark Farm & Petting Zoo
31. Parky's Farm at Winton Woods Park
32. Parky's Wet Playground - Parky's Ark at Winton Woods
33. Parky's Wet Playground - Parky's Pirate Cove at Miami Whitewater Forest

- continued

See Central Cincinnati and Newport, Kentucky map for additional attractions.

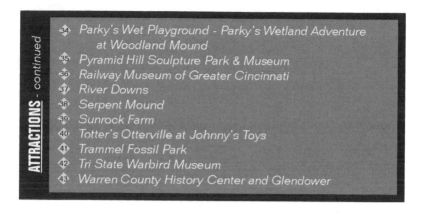

ATTRACTIONS - continued

34 Parky's Wet Playground - Parky's Wetland Adventure
    at Woodland Mound
35 Pyramid Hill Sculpture Park & Museum
36 Railway Museum of Greater Cincinnati
37 River Downs
38 Serpent Mound
39 Sunrock Farm
40 Totter's Otterville at Johnny's Toys
41 Trammel Fossil Park
42 Tri State Warbird Museum
43 Warren County History Center and Glendower

GREATER CINCINNATI

ADVENTURE STATION AT
SHARON WOODS PARK

<u>Address:</u>   11450 Lebanon Road, Sharonville, OH 45241

<u>Phone:</u>   (513) 563-4513

<u>Website:</u>   http://www.greatparks.org/rec_playgrounds/
playgrounds.shtm

<u>Hours:</u>   January–March
Tuesday–Sunday: 10 a.m.–5 p.m.

April
Daily: 10 a.m.–5 p.m.

May–Labor Day
Daily: 10 a.m.–6 p.m.

Labor Day–October
Daily: 10 a.m.–5 p.m.

November–December
Tuesday–Sunday: 10 a.m.–5 p.m.

<u>Cost:</u> $2.50 Children (2–12)
Free Parents accompanying children

Hamilton County Park District
Motor Vehicle Permit:
$3 Daily
$10 Annual

<u>Ages:</u>   2–12

<u>Stroller and wheelchair friendly:</u> Yes

<u>Length of visit:</u> 1–2 hours

Description and comments:

The Adventure Station is an indoor playground located inside Sharon Centre, in Sharon Woods Park. Most of the Adventure Station has a nature theme. Kids climb up stairs through the inside of a tree, and then play in the tree house above. They can crawl through tunnels to a giant bird's nest. Also on the upper level you will find some themed rooms. Kids pretend they are in jail, climb into a covered wagon, and sit on a saddle. They crawl through more tunnels and slide down to the main floor, where there is also a cave area. If you lose track of your kids, you won't have to climb a tree to find them. Look for a set of stairs in one of the corners. An attendant sits guard at the bottom to prevent little ones escaping without their parents. Ask the attendant about the scavenger hunt. There is a Children's Corner reserved for 2–5 year olds with a ball pit and small slide. The Adventure Station is a great place to let your kids burn some energy when the weather prevents them from playing outside. Also inside Sharon Centre is a small Nature Station, with free educational exhibits that kids will like. There are interactive exhibits including a computer quiz game and some live animals including salamanders, turtles, and a snake. Outside are picnic tables and a playground.

ANDERSON FERRY

Address: Anderson Ferry Road and Route 50 in Ohio
             4030 River Road, Constance, KY 41048

Phone: (859) 586-5007

Website: www.andersonferry.org

Hours: May–October
             Monday–Friday: 6 a.m.–9:45 p.m.
             Saturday: 7 a.m.– 9:45 p.m.
             Sunday: 9 a.m.– 9:45 p.m.

             November–April
             Monday–Friday: 6 a.m.–8 p.m.
             Saturday: 7 a.m.–8 p.m.
             Sunday: 10 a.m.–8 p.m.

Cost: $4 per car one way
             $7 round trip

Ages: All ages

Stroller and wheelchair friendly: Yes

Length of visit: < 1 hour

Description and comments:

The Anderson Ferry has continuously transported vehicles across the Ohio River since 1817. In its early days, horses on each side of the river powered the boat. Although not really a destination in itself, this is a unique way for kids to experience crossing the river. This is ideal to work into your schedule if you are traveling somewhere close to the airport or the ferry. Arrive anytime during operating hours and they will quickly transport you across the river. Drive your car right onto the boat and enjoy the short ride. Riding the ferry helps children understand how people crossed the river before there were bridges. This adventure may seem simple, but becomes something special through the eyes of a child.

THE BEACH WATERPARK

Address: 2590 Water Park Drive, Mason, OH 45040

Phone: (513) 398-7946

Website: www.thebeachwaterpark.com

Hours: Mid-May–Early September
Check website for hours

Cost: $29.99 Adults and children over 48"
$12.99 Children (48" and under)
Free Children 2 and under
$12.99 Seniors (60+)

Check website for online prices
and special packages.

Check for AAA discount.

Ages: All ages

Stroller and wheelchair friendly: Yes

Length of visit: 2 hours–all day

Description and comments:

The Beach Waterpark is an older waterpark but the kids will still have a blast. It includes a children's area with a zero-depth entry pool containing small slides and a cascading mushroom. The exit from the children's area is easy to see, so you can allow your kids to roam and not worry about them leaving without you. Children need to be 45" to ride most slides in the park. Be careful in the Lazy Miami River with your smaller children; they may be safer riding with you if it is too deep for them to touch the bottom. Rent a tube for a few dollars and ride the waves with your family in the wave pool. A favorite spot is The Pearl, an 85-degree spa-pool where you can relax in the warm water.

Older kids love the many thrilling slides available in the park. The Cliff has been rated one of the top water slides in the country and drops you five stories in three seconds! The many swift and steep water slides keep them busy all day.

Picnic tables are available outside the park if you want to pack your lunch. Guests are not permitted to bring outside food into the park. Plenty of concession stands are available with snacks, drinks, and meals. Mornings are least crowded at The Beach. After lunch the crowds generally grow larger.

In the winter, The Beach has Holiday Fest, with several attractions such as ice skating, carriage rides, and a toboggan slide. Check website for hours and prices.

BEHRINGER-CRAWFORD MUSEUM

Address: 1600 Montague Road, Covington, KY 41011

Phone: (859) 491-4003

Website: www.bcmuseum.org

Hours: Tuesday–Saturday: 10 a.m.–5 p.m.
            Sunday: 1–5 p.m.
            Closed Mondays and all national holidays

Cost: $7 Adults
            $4 Children (3–17)
            $6 Seniors (60+)

Ages: 2 and up

Stroller and wheelchair friendly: Yes

Length of visit: 1–3 hours

Description and comments:

Located in Devou Park, this museum celebrates the heritage of Northern Kentucky. Kids explore hands-on exhibits while learning about Kentucky's natural and cultural history. The museum was expanded in 2007 to include more exhibits and kid-friendly features. Upon entering, you can't miss the Kentucky streetcar, the last streetcar to run in Northern Kentucky. Visitors are not permitted to board the streetcar, but there are several passengers aboard and you can push buttons to hear their stories. There is an introductory film that is helpful to watch. Most of the film is narrated by a couple of young teens and there are computer-generated graphics, making it appealing to kids. One thing that we love about this museum is that nearly every room has a play area for young kids to keep them occupied while parents and older siblings view the exhibits. These include train tables, doll houses, and kitchen toys.

Each of the four levels has one or more themes. The first floor focuses on rails. One of our favorite exhibits is the model train display. There are nearly a dozen buttons that activate trains, trolleys, lights, and sounds. The best feature is a tunnel that goes underneath the display with bubble windows on the inside of the model so that kids (and adventurous adults) can view it from the inside. The theme of the second floor is roads. You sit in a 1959 Buick Electra convertible and watch a film at the drive-in about lifestyles of the 1950s.

The third floor is the largest floor and contains exhibits on industry, rivers, immigrants, and tourism. There is also a section for rotating exhibits. Make sure you find the famous two-headed calf and shrunken head. Kids love the Roebling Suspension Bridge and interactive packet boat exhibit that has a dress-up area. The fourth floor includes the upper deck of the packet boat, a display on airport runways, and a stuffed bear.

BIG BONE LICK STATE PARK

Address: 3380 Beaver Road, Union, KY 41091

Phone: (859) 384-3522

Website: www.parks.ky.gov/findparks/recparks/bb/

Hours: Grounds open year round
            Daylight hours

            Visitor's center:
            April–December
            Daily: 8 a.m.–4:30 p.m.

            Nature center:
            Open when staffing permits, usually weekends

Cost: Free entrance to park, visitor's center,
            and outdoor museum

            Nominal charge for nature center

            Miniature golf:
            $3.50 Adults
            $2.50 Children

Ages: All ages

Stroller and wheelchair friendly: Yes

Length of visit: 2 hours

Description and comments:

Big Bone Lick was the location of many fossil finds of large animals such as mammoths and mastodons. Now it is a place to learn about the animals that once roamed the area. Walk along a paved trail through an outdoor museum with recreated grasslands and wetlands and a life-size diorama of a bog. Near the end of the one-mile trail is a herd of bison that kids enjoy watching. There are also several unpaved hiking trails to explore. The visitor's center contains a small museum with exhibits on animal remains. A small nature center includes fossils, animal bones, plant exhibits, cultural displays about Native Americans, and artifacts found at Big Bone Lick. The park also has a playground and miniature golf course for some additional fun.

CHILO LOCK 34 PARK

Address: 521 County Park Road, Chilo, OH 45112

Phone: (513) 876-9013

Website: http://parks.clermontcountyohio.gov/Chilo.aspx

Hours: Park:
Daylight hours

Museum:
May 1–Memorial Day
Thursday–Sunday: Noon–5 p.m.
May 25–Labor Day
Sunday–Friday: Noon–5 p.m.
Saturday: 11 a.m.–5 p.m.
Labor Day–May 1
Friday–Sunday: Hours vary; call to confirm

Cost: Free

Ages: All ages

Stroller and wheelchair friendly: Yes

Length of visit: 2 hours

Description and comments:

Chilo Lock 34 Park is located on the site of a former lock and dam on the Ohio River. The visitor's center and museum explain the history of both the Ohio River and the system of locks and dams which were vital to this area. The museum has kid-friendly displays covering nature and the locks. Hear different steamboat whistles or use a handcrank to operate a model of a lock. A kids' "Touch Table" allows kids to touch objects from nature including animal skins, bones, and seed pods. Another display features stuffed wildlife.   The outdoor observation deck provides a great view of the Ohio River where you can watch barges and other boats float past you. Older children and adults should stroll through the self-guided walking tour with informative plaques placed around the park. Climb aboard the 1800s steamboat, The Jennie Wade, which resides in the park, and view historical pictures. Groups should call in advance to schedule a free educational program on The Jennie Wade. Be on the lookout for wildlife in the 1.5-acre wetland here. The park also boasts a steamboat-themed playground and picnic shelters. You will be taught the importance of the locks in the history of the river while experiencing the nature surrounding the area. Combine this visit with a hike in the adjacent Crooked Run Nature Preserve.

CINCINNATI NATURE CENTER – ROWE WOODS

Address: 4949 Tealtown Road, Milford, OH 45150

Phone: (513) 831-1711

Website: www.cincynature.org

Hours: Open daily
            Hours vary by season but always open at 8 a.m.

Cost: Daily
            $8 Adults
            $3 Children (3–12)

Ages: All ages

Stroller and wheelchair friendly: Yes

Length of visit: 2–4 hours

Description and comments:

The Cincinnati Nature Center is a beautiful, natural oasis in the Cincinnati suburbs. There are 1,025 acres of land with ponds, meadows, forests, hills, and streams. The Nature Center includes 18 miles of well marked hiking trails of varying length and difficulty. One favorite trail is the handicapped and stroller friendly All Persons Trail. The visitor's center building provides trail maps to help you explore the area. While in the visitor's center, request a backpack containing tools for junior naturalists to investigate their surroundings. Hike the Turtle Trail along the boardwalk on the edge of the pond. Remember to bring quarters for fish and turtle food in order to encourage these animals to swim over for a tasty treat! Wander along the path to Lotus Pond or Matt's Pond during the spring and summer to discover the giant bull frogs. Tread softly along the edge of the pond and try to spot the frogs before they hop into the water. It is challenging to find the bulging eyes peering out from the water. Visit the original log cabin and try to figure out which side was built most recently. Look for raccoons, deer, snakes, owls, and lots and lots of birds. Take advantage of one of several bird blinds along the trails, where you can watch the birds without them seeing you. Try out the new Nature Calls program. Carry your cell phone while you hike and call the phone number on the posted signs. Type in the code on the sign and listen to a pre-recorded message from a naturalist offering information about fossils, landforms, glaciers, and more.

Each season provides something special at Rowe Woods. During the spring admire thousands of daffodils in bloom. Pack your camera for some picturesque photos of your kids. As summer arrives, the leaves take over and change the look of the woods. Fall, of course, brings beautiful changes of colors, and winter is a fun time to bundle up (pack your boots) and hike while searching for wildlife.

Inside the Nature Center you'll find several interesting displays. Listen to various bird calls, see the length of an eagle's wing span, and understand the life and trials of migratory birds. Your children can play on the small playset, climb through a hollow log, and draw a picture for all to see. Visit live snakes and spiders on display too. Use the binoculars to admire the birds through the large viewing window and try to identify them. A gift shop has a nice selection of books, jewelry, hiking supplies, and nature-inspired art.

If you have questions about nature, animals, trees, birds, etc., be sure to ask one of the naturalists. They are extremely knowledgeable and happy to help.

Enjoy your lunch outside at a picnic table or at tables inside the Nature Center library. You will also find some cozy chairs and a fireplace in the library, too. Burn off some energy, take in some beautiful nature, and learn something on your visit to Rowe Woods.

The Fall of 2011 is the opening of the Marge and Charles Schott Nature Playscape. This is a natural play area containing several habitats focusing on nature and will promote a sense of play and wonder.

CINCINNATI/NORTHERN KENTUCKY INTERNATIONAL AIRPORT TOUR

Address: 2939 Terminal Drive, Hebron, KY 41048

Phone: (859) 767-3144

Website: www.cvgairport.com/about_us/fun_and_educational/Airport_Tours.aspx

Hours: By appointment

Cost: Free tour
Free parking

Ages: 5 and up

Stroller and wheelchair friendly: No

Length of visit: 2 hours

Description and comments:

You'll need to gather a group of at least 15 people and call at least two weeks in advance in order to take a tour of the Cincinnati/Northern Kentucky International Airport, but you will be glad you did. Kids will enjoy going into a real jet (now used for training purposes) and taking turns sitting in the cockpit and flipping switches, while the rest of the group watches an educational video. Your tour may include a visit to the airport fire department where kids learn about special equipment and training needed to fight airplane fires. Visit the police station and see the interrogation rooms and the jail cells. Another option for the tour is to visit the airfield maintenance department. The tour does not include baggage handling or airport operations, but the kids on our tour had a great time. Holscher Park is on the airport grounds and has a shelter, picnic tables, a play runway, and plenty of room for the kids to run around. Make sure everyone uses the restroom before you leave the airport because there are no restrooms at the park.

COCO KEY WATER RESORT

Address: 11320 Chester Road, Cincinnati, OH 45246

Phone: (513) 771-2080

Website: www.cocokeywaterresort.com/Locations/cincinnati

Hours: Always open Thursday–Sunday
Open Monday–Wednesday seasonally
Hours vary seasonally. Check website for details.

Cost: Day pass rates average $25 per person. Rates can be higher on peak days and lower at other times. Check website for online specials. Children 1 and under are free.

Ages: 0–12

Stroller and wheelchair friendly: Strollers and wheelchairs are permitted in the resort, but not in the water.

Length of visit: 4 hours–all day

Description and comments:

CoCo Key Water Resort is an indoor water park that is sure to please the kids. It is attached to the Sheraton North Cincinnati hotel and offers either overnight packages or day passes. There is a changing area with showers and lockers and towels are provided. Swim diapers are required. Young children gravitate toward Parrot's Perch which has small slides, an umbrella water feature, a zero-depth entry area, and water cannons. Watch out for the little ones when the giant bucket spills over. The Dip-In Theater shows animated movies or television programs on a boat sail screen. Older kids (over 48" tall) love the water slides. There are two body slides and two tube slides. They have tubes for either one or two people. Coral Reef Cavern is an activity pool where kids play water basketball or cross the pool on lily pads. Float through the resort on a tube, on the lazy river ride. Palm Grotto is a hot tub that is designated for adults, but if the park isn't busy, they will allow kids to enter with an adult. The hot tub has a swim-through passage to the outdoor hot tub. CoCo Key also has a nice arcade area with video games and skee-ball, where kids collect tickets to trade in at the redemption area. There is a Pizza Hut Express and an A&W restaurant located inside the resort.

CONEY ISLAND

Address: 6201 Kellogg Avenue, Cincinnati, OH 45228

Phone: (513) 232-8230

Website: www.coneyislandpark.com

Hours: Daily, Memorial Day–Labor Day
Sunlite Pool: 10 a.m.–8 p.m.
Classic Rides: 11 a.m.–9 p.m.
Hours may vary. Check website for schedule.

Cost: Sunlite Pool:
$11.95 Adults and children 4+ ($8.95 after 4 p.m.)
$3.95 Children (2–3)

Coney's Classic Rides:
$11.95 All Day Ride Bracelet (4+)
($8.95 after 4 p.m.)
$6.95 All Day Ride Bracelet (3 and under)

No fee to walk around the park or see shows

Sunlite Pool & Classic Rides Combo Ticket
$21.95 Adults & children 4+ ($11.95 after 4 p.m.)
$10.50 Children (2–3)

$7 Parking

Check for AAA discount.

Ages: 2 and up

Stroller and wheelchair friendly: Yes

Length of visit: 2 hours–all day

Description and comments:

Founded on June 21, 1886, Coney Island is a Cincinnati tradition. Situated on 75 acres, Coney Island has more than 50 rides and attractions, including Sunlite Pool, the world's largest recirculating swimming pool. Splash around in over an acre of shallow water. The Twister waterslide attraction opened in 2009 and has two body slides and two double-innertube slides. Kids taller than 48" can race each other down the Twister and zoom down the park's other three waterslides.

The other side of the park has 22 classic carnival-type rides, like the Scrambler, Ferris Wheel, and Tilt-A-Whirl. Adventurous riders should experience the thrill of a 50-foot freefall on The Scream Machine. Our kids love to hop on a mat and zip down the Giant Slide. Spend some time on the waters of Lake Como in a bumper boat, canoe, or pedal boat. Five rides have been designed specifically for young children under 48" tall, including the Frog Hopper and Turtle Parade. Plan to watch at least one of several live stage shows that include music, singing, and dancing. Our kids love the audience participation in the kids' shows. Small children love exploring Coney Kids Town. You'll also find a miniature golf course, craft corner, and arcade games. Coney Island hosts several festivals and special events throughout the year. Check the website for details.

CREATION MUSEUM

Address: 2800 Bullittsburg Church Road,
Petersburg, KY 41080

Phone: (888) 582-4253

Website: www.creationmuseum.org

Hours: Monday–Friday: 10 a.m.–6 p.m.
Saturday: 9 a.m.–6 p.m.
Sunday: Noon–6 p.m.

Cost: $24.95 Adults
$14.95 Children (5–12)
Free Children 4 and under
$19.95 Seniors (60+)
$7.95 Planetarium with admission

Ages: 5 and up

Stroller and wheelchair friendly: Yes

Length of visit: 2 hours–all day

Description and comments:

The Creation Museum holds 165 displays filled with scientific evidence supporting the theory of creation. The displays and films in this museum are state-of-the-art. Many of the animatronic displays were created by Patrick Marsh, who developed attractions like *Jaws* and *King Kong* at Universal Studios. Enter with an open mind and you will understand more about different ideas of how we all came to be. "Walk through Biblical History" is the main part of the museum. It is a self-guided tour including Adam and Eve, Noah's Ark, and ending with Jesus. Walk on the life-sized model of a section of Noah's Ark. You can visit the

Dinosaur Den (not handicapped accessible) and identify several dinosaurs along with a fossilized dinosaur egg and a triceratops skeleton casting.

You shouldn't miss the several professionally made films. The Stargazers Planetarium (for an additional fee) boasts digital technology and is a spectacular show you will enjoy in comfortable reclining seats. The Special Effects theater (no extra charge) was our kids' favorite show. This theater has vibrating seats and mist-spraying jets. The film about dragons and their place in both fairytales and biblical history is also intriguing.

Outside the museum is a delightful botanical garden with a mile of paved walking trails. Cross over five bridges and admire the blooming flowers and scenic waterfalls. A picnic area is available here, also. A restaurant is located inside the museum. Visit the petting zoo outside with a variety of animals including a camel, wallaby, goats, and many others. Between spending time inside the museum viewing the displays, watching the movies, having lunch, and journeying outside, a whole day of learning and fun is enjoyed by everyone.

CROOKED RUN NATURE PRESERVE

Address: 100 Crooked Run, Chilo, OH 45112

Phone: (513) 732-2977

Website: http://parks.clermontcountyohio.gov/
Crooked.aspx

Hours: Daylight hours

Cost: Free

Ages: All ages

Stroller and wheelchair friendly: Trails are flat, but unpaved

Length of visit: 2 hours

Description and comments:

The Crooked Run Nature preserve sits next to Chilo Lock 34 Park. This is a beautiful park along the Ohio River. While hiking the property, observe the birds and animals through three wildlife viewing blinds. Visitors and staff have spotted over 180 types of birds in the park. Pack your binoculars and see what you can find. Kids might want to have a notebook or a bird identification book to record their observations. The park contains over one mile of hiking trails and has scenic overlooks of the river. Restroom and picnic facilities are available. The Naturalist's office is adjacent in Chilo Lock 34 Park. Check the website for scheduled programs. Tent-like yurts are available for overnight camping; reservations required.

ENTERTRAINMENT JUNCTION

Address: 7379 Squire Court, West Chester, OH 45069

Phone: (513) 898-8000
(877) 898-4656

Website: www.entertrainmentjunction.com

Hours: Monday–Saturday: 10 a.m.–6 p.m.
Sunday: Noon–6 p.m.
January–March: Closed Wednesdays

Cost: EnterTRAINment Journey

$12.95 Adults
$9.95 Children (3–12)
Free Children 2 and under
$11.50 Seniors (65+)

A-Maze-N Funhouse

$9.95 All Ages

Seasonal attractions have additional fee; combo tickets available. Check website or AAA for discounts.

Ages: 2 and up

Stroller and wheelchair friendly: Yes

Length of visit: 2 hours

Description and comments:

Train enthusiasts relish a visit to EnterTRAINment Junction. Stroll through the world's largest indoor interactive model train display, covering three periods of railroading. Young children enjoy pushing buttons that trigger sound effects or set a train into motion. Stop at the Imagination Junction — a play area with a climbing structure, wooden train table, and video screen showing *Thomas the Tank Engine* movies. In the American Railroading Museum, learn about the evolution of locomotives, railroad lore, and how railroads affected the American culture. A display shows the actual size of a train engine wheel, but the museum does not contain any actual railway cars. Test your knowledge at interactive kiosks. EnterTRAINment Junction also includes an expo center with additional train layouts and artifacts, seasonal attractions (for an additional fee), a café, and outdoor hand crank railroad cars that operate seasonally.

New in 2011 is the A-Maze-N Funhouse. This funhouse lives up to its name with attractions like a mirror maze, curtain maze, and a claustrophobia hallway.

FORT ANCIENT

Address: 6123 State Route 350, Oregonia, OH 45054

Phone: (513) 932-4421
          (800) 283-8904

Website: http://ohsweb.ohiohistory.org/places/sw04

Hours: April–November
          Tuesday–Saturday: 10 a.m.–5 p.m.
          Sunday: Noon–5 p.m.

          December–March
          Saturday: 10 a.m.–5 p.m.
          Sunday: Noon–5 p.m.
          Call for scheduled tour starting times.

Cost: $6 Adults
          $4 Children (6–12)
          Free Children 5 and under
          $5 Seniors (60+)
          $8 Park only (no museum admission), per vehicle
          Check for AAA and discounts.

Ages: 8 and up for standard tours
          Group tours for younger children can be
          arranged with advance notice.

Stroller and wheelchair friendly: Yes

Length of visit: 1 hour for museum tour; allow extra time
to explore grounds and hike trails

Description and comments:

    Visit Fort Ancient and learn about the prehistory of
Ohio's native people. Archaeological findings range from
when the earliest people hunted mastodons with spears, to

when the Adena people became an agricultural society, and then to the time of the European settlers arriving. See tools they developed, such as an atlatl (spear-thrower) and bow and arrow, and items that were traded from as far away as South America. Learn about the earthworks and mounds built by the Hopewell culture, and find out how they were used. See the 18,000 feet of earthen walls surrounding Fort Ancient. The museum contains well-done displays and you can either walk through and read the information yourself or plan your visit around a guided tour. During a tour you may be able to try shooting an atlatl or play a game of double ball, invented by Native Americans. Visit the classroom and open drawers filled with artifacts and other items you can touch. Let your kids bang on the drum. Outside you will discover a Hopewell dwelling, a canoe, and a prehistoric garden. Archaeologists work at Fort Ancient during the summer and if you would like to see them at work on an excavation site, plan to visit in July. The grounds extend beyond the museum area and it is worth your time to see the two scenic overlooks. There are picnic areas, pit toilets, and hiking trails. Fort Ancient has both interesting learning opportunities as well as a beautiful natural setting. Older kids will appreciate the museum, but there are parts that will appeal to younger children as well.

GARDEN OF HOPE

Address: 699 Edgecliff Street, Covington, KY 41014

Phone: (859) 491-1777

Hours: Tours by appointment only
Grounds are open daylight hours
Good Friday: Open for tours, call for hours
Easter Sunrise Service: 7 a.m.

Cost: Donations appreciated

Ages: All ages

Stroller and wheelchair friendly: Stroller friendly,
but not wheelchair accessible

Length of visit: 1–2 hours

Description and comments:

The Garden of Hope is a 2.5-acre garden containing an exact replica of Jesus' tomb. An architect in Jerusalem was hired to take the exact measurements so the tomb could be replicated here. The grounds contain a small, Spanish style chapel and a carpenter's shop like the one Joseph would have worked in. The carpenter's shop includes historic tools donated by Israeli Prime Minister David Ben Gurion in 1956. The shop houses a mural depicting life in a Palestinian carpenter shop. One of the paving stones at the chapel is an actual stone from the location where Jesus preached the Sermon on the Mount. The garden includes an Italian marble statue of Jesus and authentic stones from the Good Samaritan Inn, the Jordan River, and Solomon's Temple. The grounds are landscaped with over 500 rocks, trees, and plants from Jerusalem.

Very few people in the area know about this gem of a park. Pastor Ed Kirkwood and tour guide Steve Cummins would love to have more people visit and show off the garden. The tour is interesting and you'll hear some history and explanations of the park and browse the insides of all the buildings. The view of Covington and downtown Cincinnati is spectacular from the garden. The Garden is open during the Labor Day weekend fireworks with hamburgers, hotdogs and live music...including a great view of the fireworks!

GORMAN HERITAGE FARM

Address: 10052 Reading Road, Evendale, OH 45241

Phone: (513) 563-6663

Website: www.gormanfarm.org

Hours: Wednesday–Saturday: 9 a.m.–5 p.m.
Sunday: Noon–5 p.m.
Limited winter hours. Check website for details.

Cost: $5 Adults
$3 Children (3–17)
Check local community papers or the
Cincinnati Public Libraries for discount
coupons.

Ages: All ages

Stroller and wheelchair friendly: Yes
Trails are paved, some have packed gravel.
Call ahead if you need assistance; they will arrange to have you park to avoid the gravel or they will transport you in a golf cart.

Length of visit: 1–4 hours

Description and comments:

Come visit the farm and see and learn about a variety of farm animals. When you arrive, pick up scavenger hunt questions (or find them on the website) to keep your kids focused and interested. You'll see and learn about chickens, cows, donkeys, horses, pigs, rabbits, sheep, goats, and a turkey. You'll also understand the uses of the farm machinery like combines and tractors while also exploring the buildings on the property. Notice the building with bars on the window made from old wagon wheels. Visit the Children's Garden and see herbs, sunflowers, fruit trees, and a sundial. Learn the reasons to keep a compost pile and what should go into them. If you're lucky, you might catch a glimpse of a hummingbird!

Gorman Heritage Farm sits on 122 acres of land right off of I-75. Visiting the farm allows children to see where their food and farm products originate. They will see freshly laid eggs and wool being sheared from a sheep. Take a hike along a trail (one is stroller/handicap accessible) to see the wildlife in the pond and the trees in the Old Growth Forest.

Gorman has several camps and festivals throughout the year. Check the website for more information.

Wear comfortable shoes, pack sunscreen, a water bottle, and bug spray, and be ready to experience life on the farm in the middle of Cincinnati.

GRANT BOYHOOD HOME AND SCHOOLHOUSE

Address: Grant Boyhood Home:
219 East Grant Avenue, Georgetown, OH 45121

Grant Schoolhouse:
508 South Water Street, Georgetown, OH 45121

Phone: (937) 378-3087

Website: Grant Boyhood Home:
http://ohsweb.ohiohistory.org/places/sw09

Grant Schoolhouse:
http://ohsweb.ohiohistory.org/places/sw10

Hours: Memorial Day–Labor Day
Wednesday–Sunday: Noon–5 p.m.

September and October
Saturday and Sunday: Noon–5 p.m.
Closed holidays

Cost: One price for both sites:
$3 Adults
$1 Children (6–12)
Free Children 5 and under

Ages: 4 and up

Stroller and wheelchair friendly: No

Length of visit: 1 hour

Description and comments:

Ohio is known as the "Mother of Presidents," and there are several sites of presidential significance near Cincinnati. Two of these are the home and schoolhouse where Ulysses

S. Grant spent his early childhood. Start at Grant's Boyhood Home, where you can learn about Grant's upbringing as well as see a typical rural home of the 1800s. Kids will be captivated by the animatronic display of Ulysses at the age of 15 as he discusses his aspirations. You can touch metal objects to activate the display and hear him talk about their significance in his life. There are displays of historical artifacts including the binoculars that Grant used during the Civil War. Walk or drive a few blocks from the boyhood home to the one-room schoolhouse where Grant's formal education began. Both sites are operated under the same management. At the schoolhouse, you will learn how school was conducted with students of all ages in the same classroom. According to our tour guide, this schoolhouse produced four admirals and two generals, in addition to Ulysses S. Grant who was both a general and president.

HERITAGE VILLAGE MUSEUM
AT SHARON WOODS PARK

Address: 11450 Lebanon Road, Sharonville, OH 45241

Phone: (513) 563-9484

Website: www.heritagevillagecincinnati.org

Hours: May–September
           Wednesday–Saturday: 10 a.m.–5 p.m.
           Sunday: 1–5 p.m.

           Tour Times
           Wednesday–Friday: 10:30 a.m., 12:45 p.m., 3 p.m.
           Saturday: 10:30 a.m., 12 p.m., 1:30 p.m., 3 p.m.
           Sunday: 1:30 p.m., 2:15 p.m., 3 p.m.

           Open other dates throughout the year for special
           events.

Cost: $5 Adults
           $3 Children (5–11)
           Free Children 4 and under

           Hamilton County Park District
           Motor Vehicle Permit:
           $3 Daily
           $10 Annual

Ages: 3 and up

Stroller and wheelchair friendly: Almost completely

Length of visit: 1–3 hours

Description and comments:

   Heritage Village Museum is a collection of about a dozen
historic buildings that depict life as it was in the 19th century.

The buildings dating from 1804 to 1891 were rescued from destruction and moved from other locations in the region to recreate a village setting. There are four homes, a summer kitchen, a barn, medical office, mercantile store, print shop, church, one-room schoolhouse, and a train station. During regular operating hours, a tour guide takes you through the buildings. They will usually have at least one demonstration for you to view, such as butter churning or candle dipping. Heritage Village has several special events and programs throughout the year. During special events, there are interpreters in every building with many demonstrations throughout the village. Check the website for dates and prices of special events.

If you plan to attend with a group, call ahead to request that they open the Hands On History Center. Kids ages ten and under love this area where they touch and interact with items that are typically off limits in historic homes. They can recline on an antique bed, pretend to cook at an antique stove, and play with a variety of old-fashioned toys.

HIGHFIELD DISCOVERY GARDEN AT GLENWOOD GARDENS PARK

Address: 10397 Springfield Pike, Cincinnati, OH 45215

Phone: (513) 771-8733

Website: http://greatparks.org/discoverygarden/index. shtm

Hours: April–October
Tuesday–Saturday: 9:30 a.m.–5 p.m.
Sunday: Noon–5 p.m.

November–March
Wednesday–Saturday: 9:30 a.m.–5 p.m.
Sunday: Noon–5 p.m.

Cost: $7 Adults
$5 Children (2–12)
Free Children 1 and under,
with accompanying adult

Discounted rates during off season. Family season passes available.

Hamilton County Park District
Motor Vehicle Permit:
$3 Daily
$10 Annual

Ages: 3–8

Stroller and wheelchair friendly: Yes

Length of visit: 2–4 hours

Description and comments:

Within the pastoral Glenwood Gardens park, you'll find

Highfield Discovery Garden. This park is perfect for kids ages 3–8. Younger kids in strollers will also have a great time visiting the park. Kids will climb in the 25-foot tall Discovery Tree, designed with kids in mind. They will explore inside the trunk, view the park from the branches and hunt for hidden animals within the tree. The Discovery Tree and the whole park are fully accessible for physically challenged visitors. Grandma's Scent Garden was designed for the visually impaired. Many different textures of trees and plants can be felt, and the aroma of the flowers and herbs in this garden will delight everyone. Grandma has a play house complete with table and chairs waiting for a tea party.

The Wizard's Garden includes a boardwalk, a swinging bridge, and a dragon! Fallen trees in the park have been sculpted into some interesting characters. Walk along the hillside and see if you can spot them.

Supplies are available to water the many growing plants in the Vegetable Garden. Train enthusiasts will want to step into the Trolley Garden where the miniature locomotive travels through several familiar storybook scenes.

On your visit to the Butterfly Garden you'll see it is shaped like its namesake. Flowers and plants which attract butterflies are plentiful here. Frog and Toad's Pond contains several varieties of fish, frogs, and dragonflies.

Highfield Discovery Garden has educational programs with themes that change every two weeks. Programs take place at 10:45 a.m., 1 p.m., and 4 p.m. on Wednesday–Saturday, and 1 p.m. and 4 p.m. on Sunday.

These gardens are vibrant, entertaining, and educational, too. While here, don't forget to discover the rest of Glenwood Gardens. A scenic overlook in the park has views of rolling meadows and open woodlands. You will find stroller- friendly paths in the park too. There are no picnic tables available, only some park benches inside of Glenwood Gardens. Bring a large blanket with you and enjoy your picnic on the lawn.

IRONS FRUIT FARM

Address: 1640 Stubbs Mill Road, Lebanon, OH 45036

Phone: (513) 932-2853

Website: www.ironsfruitfarm.com

Hours: June–October
Monday–Saturday: 9 a.m.–6 p.m.
Sunday: Noon–5 p.m.

Cost: Fruit is priced by weight or volume

Ages: All ages

Stroller and wheelchair friendly: No

Length of visit: 1–2 hours

Description and comments:

Pick your own berries, apples, gourds, or pumpkins. Start at the market building, where a farm employee will give you baskets and send you off into the field. Our kids love this! Always call ahead to inquire if fruit is ready to be picked because the supply is limited. Blueberries generally ripen mid-June to mid-July, apples from mid-September to early October, and pumpkins late September through October. Your kids may also feed the farm animals and play on a swing set. The farm has a market, a bakery, and picnic tables onsite. On weekends in October, there are hayrides and a corn maze.

JUNGLE JIM'S INTERNATIONAL MARKET

<u>Address:</u>   5440 Dixie Highway, Fairfield, OH 45014

<u>Phone:</u>   (513) 674-6000
         (513) 674-6023 for tours

<u>Website:</u>   www.junglejims.com

<u>Hours:</u>   Daily: 8 a.m.–10 p.m.
         Tours are scheduled on weekdays only

<u>Cost:</u>   Tours
         $5 Adults and children
         Jungle Jim's $2 coupon included
         with price of tour

<u>Ages:</u>   Store visit: all ages
         Tour best for kids 4 and up

<u>Stroller and wheelchair friendly:</u> Yes

<u>Length of visit:</u> Tours last 1 ½ hours
                 Shopping: allow 1–2 hours minimum

<u>Description and comments:</u>

Jungle Jim's International Market is an amazing grocery store that has been featured on *Food Network, Good Morning America, Time Magazine, Cincinnati Magazine*, and many more. They carry unique and authentic foods, beer, and wines from all over the world. Pulling into the parking lot you'll notice the waterfall, pond, and the life-sized plaster giraffes, elephants, monkeys, and a gorilla all waiting to welcome you to this unique shopping experience. The store is decorated with lots of kid-friendly themes. You'll spot an animated lion dressed like Elvis singing every five minutes. A 5 ½-foot tall Campbell's Soup Can Man swings over the soup aisle. Watch and listen to the animatronic displays like Pedro the Mariachi Man, some chirping Birdies, and a band featuring Lucky the Leprechaun, Trix the Rabbit, and the Cheerios Honey Bee, all playing 50's tunes. You'll even find a 1952 fire truck perched over the 1,000 varieties of hot sauce. There is also a theatre with a movie explaining the story behind Jungle Jim's. Make sure you visit Sherwood Forest and Robin Hood in the English foods section. Above your head is a 30-foot tree. Look up while under the tree and you'll see lots of surprises! Find the giant fish pond and pick out something to take home for dinner. A trip to Jungle Jim's isn't complete without a trip to the award winning bathrooms. From the outside, they appear to be simple portable toilets, but on the inside, they open to nice modern bathrooms.

The tour is an educational addition to your shopping trip. Be sure to arrange this in advance. The tour takes you throughout the store and a guide explains several interesting foods and facts. Learn behind-the-scenes information while tasting many delicious samples. You'll see odd foods like sheep heads and duck feet. Dinner, anyone?

At print time, a second Jungle Jim's store is under construction in Eastgate. It is expected to open in early 2012.

KINGS ISLAND AND BOOMERANG BAY WATERPARK

Address: 6300 Kings Island Drive,
             Kings Island, OH 45034

Phone: (513) 754-5700

Website: www.visitkingsisland.com

Hours: Mid-April–Early November
             Check website for operating hours and days
             Closed to the public most of September

Cost: $35.99 Adults and children 48" and taller
             (online price)

             $51.99 Adults and children 48" and taller
             (regular price)

             $31.99 Children 3 and up, under 48" tall
             (online price)

             Free Children 2 and under

Ages: All ages
             Must be at least 36" tall to ride most rides
             in Planet Snoopy

Stroller and wheelchair friendly: Yes

Length of visit: 2 hours–all day

Description and comments:

    Amusement Today readers have voted Kings Island's kids' area as the best in the world. The kids' area makes its debut as the newly themed "Planet Snoopy" in 2010, with PEANUTS-themed rides. Your children will be thrilled experiencing the rides in Planet Snoopy if they are at least

36 inches tall. This area includes 18 attractions featuring four kid roller coasters. The rides allow kids to fly in the air, chug down the tracks, and swing around. You will never forget the smiles on your kids' faces.

If your kids have graduated from Planet Snoopy, but are not quite ready for The Beast roller coaster, there are many other options in the park for the not-quite-so adventurous. Verify thrill levels and height restrictions for all the rides on the park map. A height of 48" allows guests the option of experiencing many more rides in the park. Some of our favorites are The Beast (the world's longest wooden roller coaster); Delirium; Vortex; Drop Zone; FireHawk; and Shake, Rattle & Roll. Diamondback and Windseeker are the newest thrill rides in the park.

See a variety of high quality shows for children and adults. The shows feature singing, dancing, and ice skating. The dancing fountains at the entrance to the park are also a favorite. Don't forget to ride the elevator up the Eiffel Tower to scan the park from above.

When you need to cool off, take the train to Boomerang Bay, the water park at Kings Island. (Only season passholders may use the parking lot entrance.) Smaller kids enjoy their own special area with a zero-depth-entry pool, a mini slide, and a cascading mushroom. There is a raft ride specially designed for a child and a parent. Float on the Crocodile Run lazy river and ride the waves in the 36,000 square foot wave pool. There are plenty more exciting rides for bigger kids and parents looking for some adventure. Be sure swimsuits don't have exposed zippers, buckles, rivets, drain holes, or metal ornamentation since these are not allowed on the water slides. Boomerang Bay is fun on its own or paired with a day at Kings Island. For the little ones, we recommend choosing one park and spending the day there. Either park could be an entire day's event.

Be aware that visitors are not permitted to bring coolers into the park. You can eat your lunch on the picnic tables outside the main entrance. Another option is to pack lawn chairs in your vehicle and dine in comfort at your car. Concession stands are also located inside the park. Any concession stand will gladly provide cups of ice water so go ahead and leave your water bottle at home.

New in 2011 is Dinosaurs Alive!, the world's largest animatronic dinosaur park, with more than 60 life-sized dinosaur models in an outdoor forest setting. This attraction has a separate admission fee.

LEBANON MASON MONROE RAILROAD

Address: Lebanon Station:
127 South Mechanic Street, Lebanon, OH 45036

Mason Station:
5660 Tylersville Road, Mason, OH 45040

Phone: (513) 933-8022

Website: www.lebanonrr.com

Hours: Operates most weekends during spring,
summer, and fall and some Wednesdays and
Fridays during the summer. Also operates
during Christmas season. Check website for
operating schedule.

Cost: One hour train ride:
$13 Adults
$8 Children (5–16)
$5 Children (2–4)
Free Children 1 and under
$8 Seniors

Weekend themed events are priced separately.
Check website for details.

LM&M recommends purchasing
all tickets in advance.

Ages: All ages

Stroller and wheelchair friendly: No, but foldaway
wheelchairs and strollers can be stowed.

Length of visit: 1–2 hours

Description and comments:

Enjoy the scenic beauty of the Warren County countryside from aboard a vintage train. Lebanon Mason Monroe (LM&M) Railroad operates one-hour train rides, during which you can learn about railroad history and operation, or simply enjoy the ride from either your passenger coach or the open-air gondola. Railroad conductors have a wealth of knowledge to share. Many family-friendly events are scheduled on weekends throughout the year, with themes such as Curious George, Thomas the Tank Engine, and Pumpkin Patch Express.

The trains are not currently heated or air-conditioned, so dress appropriately. There are restrooms at the train station, but not on the train. Plan to arrive 45 minutes in advance of the scheduled departure time in order to park, pick up tickets, and use the restroom. Boarding begins 15 minutes prior to the departure time. Make sure you have cash if you would like to purchase food on the train.

LITTLE MIAMI BIKE TRAIL

Address: Milford to Urbana, along the Little Miami River

Website: www.littlemiamibiketrail.com

Hours: Daylight hours

Cost: Free

Ages: All ages

Stroller and wheelchair friendly: Yes

Length of visit: 2–4 hours

Description and comments:

This paved bike trail follows the picturesque Little Miami River, a federal and state scenic river. Charming stores and unique refreshment stands can be found along the trail. Walk, bike, rollerblade, ride your horse, or even cross country ski on the 72-mile trail. The trail intersects with roads and inactive railroad crossings, so you will want to pay close attention to your smaller riders to keep them safe. Bike rental locations dot the trail along the way. Check the website for a map of the trail, bike rental information, and lists of restaurants at stops along the way.

The trail passes through Loveland at Nisbet Park. Take a short walk down the hill and through the woods behind the playground where you will find the river. This is the perfect spot to wade into the water and hunt for fossils among the rocks. While in Loveland, visit Pizazz Studio, a charming gift shop in Loveland where your kids can shop for Webkinz. Loveland Sweets is available to tame your sweet tooth with cookies, candy, and ice cream. Paxton's Grill is a family-friendly local eatery, and The Works serves brick oven pizzas and has plenty of space.

Some other notable stops along the trail include Camp Dennison (milepost 1.3) which was a Volunteer Recruiting Service for training of Union troops before the Civil War. Fort Ancient (see separate listing) is at milepost 26.6 and the Birthplace of Tecumseh (milepost 53.7) is where this great Shawnee leader had his beginnings.

LOVELAND CASTLE - CHATEAU LAROCHE

Address: 12025 Shore Road, Loveland, OH 45140

Phone: (513) 683-4686

Website: www.lovelandcastle.com

Hours: April–September
Daily: 11 a.m.–5 p.m.

October–March (Weather Permitting)
Saturday and Sunday: 11 a.m.–5 p.m.

Cost: $3 per person

Ages: 2 and up

Stroller and wheelchair friendly: No

Length of visit: 1–2 hours

Description and comments:

One of Cincinnati's most unique attractions, the Loveland Castle, or Chateau LaRoche, was the dream of one man, Harry Andrews, and his Boy Scout troop (named the Knights of the Golden Trail). It was built to resemble a medieval European Castle. Taking advantage of its location on the Little Miami River, Andrews used rocks from the river and bricks he made himself to construct the castle. The Knights of the Golden Trail organization is still in existence and its primary activity is operating the castle. On your visit, you learn more about the castle construction and its features. Watch the video about Harry Andrews and his time building the castle. Look for the rocks in the wall that have come from places all over the world. Investigate the design of the front door, and then inquire about how it could keep out intruders. Descend to the basement and check out the dungeon. Plan to spend time exploring the beautiful gardens. Don't forget your camera! Take advantage of a great backdrop for some photographs of the kids. Next, wander down to the river. This is a great spot for a picnic lunch. Note that there are two portable restrooms, but no indoor restrooms. Also, the circular stairs in the castle are steep and narrow and will make the parent of a young toddler nervous. Preschoolers and school-age children will have fun exploring the castle.

MARIEMONT BELL TOWER CARILLON

Address: Pleasant Street, Mariemont, OH 45227

Phone: Contact Dick Gegner for tours
(513) 271-8519

Website: www.mariemontpreservation.org/tours.htm

Hours: Tours by appointment only

Cost: Free

Ages: 3 and up

Stroller and wheelchair friendly: No

Length of visit: 1 hour (allow extra time to play at the park)

Description and comments:

Tucked away along Route 50 in the charming and historic town of Mariemont is Dogwood Park. Within Dogwood Park is a wonderful surprise, the Bell Tower Carillon. A carillon is a musical instrument that contains at least 23 large bells. The Bell Tower Carillon in Mariemont is 100 feet high and contains 49 bells covering four different octaves. Call about a week in advance and schedule a tour of this amazing landmark.

To begin this tour you will ride an old and small elevator to the room where the carillon is played. You might need to board the elevator in shifts of 3–4 people. The carillon is small and only holds about 6–8 people at once. The carillonneur will explain the history of the tower and play a song to demonstrate how the notes are played. You'll be amazed at the amount of strength and talent it takes to play a melody. Next, climb about 12 steps up to view the bells in the tower. Examine the two-ton bell "Bourdon" and all the other bells that make up this musical instrument. Your tour guide will stay downstairs and will play some of the different bells so you can watch, feel, and hear the vibrations and sound of these large bells. The Bell Tower Carillon has recently undergone major renovations; the facilities are updated and a little roomier than before.

Concerts are held every Sunday and on holidays. Hear the concert at 7 p.m. during the summer and at 4 p.m. during the winter. On holidays the carillon plays at 2 p.m. The first Sunday in August is always a special concert for kids. Bring some lawn chairs or a blanket and enjoy.

Be sure to pack a lunch and take advantage of the picnic tables at Dogwood Park. The Tot Lot entertains with two playsets. The mature trees comfortably shade the park, keeping it cool on hot summer days. The highlight of the park for our kids is the amazing climbing trees. They are low to the ground and have scores of crooked branches all within easy reach. Even small kids can climb into these trees and feel like they are in their own tree fort. Dogwood Park also has nature trails to explore.

MEGALAND AT COLERAIN PARK

Address: 4725 Springdale Road, Cincinnati, OH 45251

Phone: (513) 385-7503

Website: www.coleraintwp.org/colerain_park.cfm

Hours: Daily: Daylight hours

Cost: Free

Ages: 2–10

Stroller and wheelchair friendly: Yes

Length of visit: 1–2 hours

Description and comments:

Megaland is a large, community-built playground inside Colerain Park. This is a special, out-of-the-ordinary park. It is a wooden playground with lots of places to climb, slide, and play. Zip lines, multi-level climbing structures, curvy slides and more keep kids busy for hours. It has many features that are different from the average playground. It is a great place to visit with kids who have lots of extra energy. The park also has picnic tables, shelters and a one-mile walking trail.

METAMORA, INDIANA

Address: Metamora, IN 47030

Phone: (765) 647-6512

Website: www.metamoraindiana.com

Hours: Gristmill
            April–Mid-December
            Wednesday–Sunday: 9 a.m.–5 p.m.

            Canal boat rides
            May–October
            Wednesday–Sunday: hourly, Noon–4 p.m.

Cost: Canal boat rides
            $4 Adults
            $2 Children (4–11)
            Free Children 3 and under
            $3.50 Seniors (55+)

Ages: 3 and up

Stroller and wheelchair friendly: Yes

Length of visit: 2–4 hours

Description and comments:

   Visiting Metamora, Indiana, takes you a step back in time. Metamora is an 1838 canal town that contains Indiana's oldest operating water-powered grist mill. Visit the mill and examine the method used to separate the wheat or corn into differing grain sizes. You can purchase their freshly ground products and take them home and bake some fresh corn bread. Be sure to refrigerate or freeze your cornmeal. It has a short shelf life without preservatives.

The canal boat ride is the other feature the kids will remember. The boat ride, powered by horses, transports passengers along the canal and over the aqueduct. The purpose of the aqueduct is to carry canal water over an existing waterway. This is the only remaining wooden aqueduct in the United States. Your captain will explain the history of how the canals were built, how Indiana paid for them, and how they were made obsolete by the railroads. See the graffiti on the inside of the aqueduct, some of which has been there for many years. After the ride, your kids will have a chance to visit and pet the horses.

Feed the ducks along the river and then dine at one of the many restaurants for lunch. Candy, fudge, and ice cream stores will keep the kids happy, too. You will find an abundance of gift and antique stores in Metamora; just be careful if you take little ones into these shops. Many are located in historic buildings and have tight spaces and breakable merchandise on low shelves. The stores are open according to their own schedules. Check the website for a list of stores and their operating hours.

If you're interested in other activities, a 2.6-mile hiking and biking trail stretches along the canal. Check the website for information on carriage rides and horseback riding in the area. Between shopping, eating, seeing the gristmill, and taking a canal boat ride, you will have a full day ahead of you in Metamora.

NOAH'S ARK FARM & PETTING ZOO

NOW CLOSED

This attraction was permanently closed in 2010

Address: 3269 Koehler Road, California, KY 41007

Phone: (859) 635-0803

Website: www.noahsarkfarmzoo.com

Hours: Wednesday–Sunday: 10 a.m.–6 p.m.
Daily in October: 10 a.m.–6 p.m.
Closed November–Mid-April

Cost: $5 per person

Ages: All ages

Stroller and wheelchair friendly: No

Length of visit: 2 hours

Description and comments:

Is your family interested in seeing familiar and unique animals up close? Noah's Ark Farm & Petting Zoo is the place for you! Drive about 30 minutes south of Cincinnati and you'll find this entertaining attraction. Take a self-guided tour around the farm. Information explaining the animals is clearly posted to make your experience interesting and educational. Purchase food for the adult animals and inquire about bottle feeding the babies. The list of animals you will meet on the farm includes five different kinds of cattle (including zebu and watusi), six kinds of sheep, and eight kinds of goats. There are llamas, emus, horses, ponies, and buffalo. Find out what a zedonk and a mara are, and see the yak, donkey, rabbits, guinea pigs, ferrets, hedgehog, chicks, ducks, turtles, exotic chickens, turkeys, peacocks, doves, pigs, dogs, and kittens. A talking parrot and a horse that answers questions are both residents of the farm. Be on the lookout for new animal additions to the farm when you visit, too.

We had the chance to hold several of the smaller animals. Haven't you always wanted to hold a hedgehog? Be certain kids are gentle when holding the animals. Take your time looking around and stay in each area as long as you like. The goats have their own playset to climb on and you might be lucky and see one slip down the slide! A real houseboat has been transformed into a play area for the goats and the children. The up-close views of the animals can't be beat and you'll surely have fond memories seeing some truly unique and interesting animals.

At the end of your visit, enjoy your lunch at the picnic area located next to the pond. Don't forget to pack your lunch because there are no snacks for sale on site. There is a portable restroom and hand-washing station available. Consider bringing some hand sanitizer with you for convenience.

PARKY'S FARM AT WINTON WOODS PARK

Address: 10073 Daly Road, Cincinnati, OH 45231

Phone: (513) 521-3276

Website: www.greatparks.org/parks/parkysfarm.shtm

Hours: Open daily
           Pony Rides, Wagon Rides and PlayBarn are
           available during select times:

           Spring and Fall
           Friday: 10 a.m.–4 p.m.
           Saturday: 11 a.m.–6 p.m.
           Sunday: Noon–6 p.m.

           Summer
           Monday–Friday: 10 a.m.–5 p.m.
           Saturday: 11 a.m.–6 p.m.
           Sunday: Noon–6 p.m.

Cost: $2.50 Pony Rides
           $2.50 Parky's PlayBarn
           $2.50 Wagon Rides

           Hamilton County Park District
           Motor Vehicle Permit:
           $3 Daily
           $10 Annual

Ages: All ages
           PlayBarn (2–12)
           Must be 48" or shorter to ride ponies

Stroller and wheelchair friendly: Yes

Length of visit: 2–4 hours

Description and comments:

Parky's Farm is great fun for young children. Part of Winton Woods Park, Parky's Farm is a 100-acre demonstration farm with orchards, gardens, and live animals including goats, pigs, sheep, and chickens. Stroll around the farm to look at the animals. If a staff member is available, kids might be able to get up close to the animals. Kids love the PlayBarn, an old dairy barn that was converted into a two-story indoor playground with a farm theme. Outside the PlayBarn you'll find kid-sized, pedal-operated John Deere wagons that kids can drive around.

Parky's Farm also has pony rides and wagon rides for an additional fee. Picnic areas and an outdoor playground are also available. On most Fridays from May through October, Parky's has Fantastic Farm Fridays with additional activities that vary with the season. In the spring, kids might be able to try milking a goat or watch a sheep being sheared. In the fall, they might visit a pumpkin patch. Parky's Farm hosts several special events each year. Sign up for the free e-mail newsletter from the Hamilton County Park District to receive information about special events.

PARKY'S WET PLAYGROUNDS

Address: Parky's Ark at Winton Woods
10245 Winton Road, Cincinnati, OH 45231

Parky's Pirate Cove at Miami Whitewater Forest
9001 Mt. Hope Road, Harrison, OH 45030

Parky's Wetland Adventure at Woodland Mound
8250 Old Kellogg Road, Cincinnati, OH 45255

Phone: (513) 521-7275

Website: www.greatparks.org/rec_playgrounds/
wetplaygrounds.shtm

Hours: Memorial Day through Labor Day
Daily: 11 a.m.–7 p.m.

Cost: $2 Children (2–12)
Free Adults and children 1 and under

Hamilton County Park District
Motor Vehicle Permit:
$3 Daily
$10 Annual

Ages: 1–7

Stroller and wheelchair friendly: Yes

Length of visit: 1–3 hours

Description and comments:

Wet playgrounds are located within three different Hamilton County Parks. Each different playground is uniquely decorated with various animals and trees spraying and squirting water. Small slides, giant turtles, and tipping coconuts are all part of the fun! There is no standing water, so it's safe for the little ones. A separate area is fenced to keep visitors ages three and under safe. You and your children should wear swimsuits because everyone will be sure to get wet. Babies and toddlers need to wear swim diapers. Kids will go crazy playing in the dancing fountains and the cascading mushroom waterfalls. Pack your lunch (picnic facilities are available in the park) or buy a treat from the snack bar. There are plenty of restroom facilities and changing areas. Bring your sunscreen and prepare to wear the kids out.

PYRAMID HILL SCULPTURE PARK
& MUSEUM

Address: 1763 Hamilton-Cleves Road, State Route 128,
            Hamilton, OH 45013

Phone: (513) 887-9514

Website: www.pyramidhill.org

Hours: April–October
            Monday–Friday: 8 a.m.–5 p.m.
            Saturday and Sunday: 8 a.m.–6 p.m.

            November–March (Weather Permitting)
            Monday–Friday: 8 a.m.–5 p.m.
            Saturday and Sunday: 10 a.m.–5 p.m.

Cost: $8 Adults
            $2 Children (5–12)
            Free Children 4 and under

Ages: All ages

Stroller and wheelchair friendly: Some trails are
accessible, but most sculptures can be viewed from vehicle.
Restrooms are accessible.

Length of visit: 1–2 hours

Description and comments:

Pyramid Hill combines the beauty of nature with
sculptural art. This is an attraction that we suggest you
visit with an open mind. You will find a wide array of huge
sculptures made from steel, granite, bronze, aluminum,
polychrome, wood and more. Some are natural, some
painted, and some polished. All are interesting and unique.
Walk right up to the sculptures, touch them, and even

walk through them. Children may not be interested in the sculptures or they may love them. The park is situated on 265 acres with both paved roads and hiking trails throughout. The park also offers gardens, lakes, and picnic facilities. Special programs for children are conducted during the summer; check the website for details.

RAILWAY MUSEUM OF GREATER CINCINNATI

Address: 315 W. Southern Avenue, Covington, KY 41015

Website: www.cincirailmuseum.org

Hours: Saturday: 10 a.m.–4 p.m.

Cost: $4 Adults
$2 Children (10 and under)
Groups larger than 12 should contact the
museum office

Ages: 3 and up

Stroller and wheelchair friendly: No

Length of visit: 1–2 hours

Description and comments:

The Railway Museum of Greater Cincinnati is a life-sized train museum. There are no model trains here: it's a genuine railroad yard with actual train cars. Leave the stroller at home. The train yard has tracks and contains many obstacles. Junior engineers view Pullman cars from 1911–1929 and sit at the controls of a Diesel locomotive. An overnight train includes a locomotive, post office, baggage, sleeping, and observation cars. Train lovers will be thrilled to stroll along the tracks and examine these cars up close. Museum volunteers are available and willing to answer questions. Upon entering, you'll receive a walking tour map to help you navigate the museum. A shaded picnic area is located on the property.

RIVER DOWNS

Address: 6301 Kellogg Avenue, Cincinnati, Ohio 45230

Phone: (513) 232-8000

Website: www.riverdowns.com

Hours: Mid-April–Labor Day
Daily, except Monday and Wednesday

Races start around 1 or 2 p.m. and last until
5:30 or 6 p.m. Check website for schedule.

Free pony rides on Saturday from 1:30–4:30 p.m.

Cost: Free
$1 for a program

Ages: 3 and up

Stroller and wheelchair friendly: Yes

Length of visit: 1–3 hours

Description and comments:

Horses have been racing at River Downs since 1925. River Downs has a one-mile track and a grandstand that seats 8,500 people and does not charge for admission or parking. You are welcome to sit and watch the races without placing any bets. On weekdays sit anywhere, even in the box seats. Walk over to the paddock area to see the horses and jockeys up close. Observe the horses being saddled before a race. Watch the jockeys walk the horses to the track for their race. Walk down to the fence and watch a race up close. As an alternative, watch the horses during their daily morning workouts which are every morning from sunrise until 10 a.m. River Downs offers free pony rides on Saturdays from 1:30–4:30 p.m. They have a concession stand and a restaurant if you want to have lunch there. Once a year River Downs holds a wiener dog race. Check the website for details. Consider renting a movie such as Dreamer so that your children can learn more about what it takes to raise a racehorse.

SERPENT MOUND

Address: 3850 State Route 73, Peebles, OH 45660

Phone: (937) 587-2796
(800) 752-2757

Website: http://ohsweb.ohiohistory.org/places/sw16/

Hours: Park Grounds:
Daily: daylight hours

Museum:
March
Saturday and Sunday: 10 a.m.–5 p.m.

April and May
Saturday and Sunday: 10 a.m.–5 p.m.
Holidays: Noon–5 p.m.

Memorial Day–Labor Day
Daily: 10 a.m.–5 p.m.
Holidays: Noon–5 p.m.

September and October
Saturday and Sunday: 10 a.m.–5 p.m.
Holidays: Noon–5 p.m.

Cost: Free admission
$7 Parking
Check for AAA discount.

Ages: 3 and up

Stroller and wheelchair friendly: Yes

Length of visit: 1 hour

Description and comments:

Serpent Mound is one of the earthworks built by prehistoric Native Americans. In the shape of a coiled serpent, the earthwork is about three feet high and over 1,300 feet long. It is believed to have been built by the Fort Ancient culture, although there are Adena burial mounds located nearby. The purpose of the mound is unknown, but it has been determined that it was not used for burial and that the head is aligned to the sunset of the summer solstice. Visitors are not permitted to climb on the mound, but can walk on a paved path around it. Climb the 35-foot tower to get a better view of the serpent design. The grounds also include a wigwam model and a Native American garden planted with corn, beans, squash, and gourds.

Additionally, the park includes a museum. One exhibit explores different theories about the meaning of the design. A model shows how the Adena burial mounds were constructed. A timeline shows all the prehistoric cultures of Ohio, and artifacts associated with each culture are displayed. Another exhibit is about the geology of the area.

SUNROCK FARM

Address: 103 Gibson Lane, Wilder, KY 41076

Phone: (859) 781-5502

Website: www.sunrockfarm.org

Hours: By reservation only
Open every day except Christmas and
New Years Day

Cost: $10 Adults and children

Ages: 2–18

Stroller and wheelchair friendly: Gravel or grass paths, large-wheeled strollers are best

Length of visit: 2 hours

Description and comments:

Do you have a young farmer or animal lover in your family? Sunrock Farm will provide a tour of their farm to groups of 8-10 people. They may be able to match you up with another family or two if you don't have enough people for a tour. The tour provides several hands-on experiences including milking a goat, holding baby chicks, gathering eggs, bottle feeding baby sheep or goats (if they are available), brushing horses, and visiting the oxen, emu, and alpaca. Plenty of great photo opportunities are available. Your kids will understand how the farm works, while seeing and touching the animals. Portable restrooms and hand-washing stations are available. Picnic tables are not available for family tours.

TOTTER'S OTTERVILLE AT JOHNNY'S TOYS

Address: 4314 Boron Drive, Covington, KY 41015

Phone: (859) 491-1441

Website: www.johnnystoys.com

Hours: Monday–Thursday: 10 a.m.–5 p.m.
           Friday and Saturday: 10 a.m.–8 p.m.
           Sunday: 11 a.m.–5 p.m.
           Closed some holidays

Cost: $7.95 Children (9 months–10 years)
           Free Children 9 months and younger
           Free Adults
           Annual passes and value passes available

Ages: 8 and under

Stroller and wheelchair friendly: Yes

Length of visit: 2–4 hours

Description and comments:

Totter's Otterville is a magical world designed specifically for kids. Enter the gates where you'll be given a bracelet with a number that matches your child's so they can't escape without you. Choose from over 25 fun and educational activities both indoors and outdoors. Outside you'll find a train to ride on, squirting fire hydrants, a maze, and a fishing area with magnetic fish. Dig for dinosaur bones or work on a construction site. Inside are several areas for creative and pretend play. A special area for kids under age three contains soft and colorful toys. See a puppet show, make a craft, or paint your face. Dress-up clothes are provided for kids to pretend they are ballerinas, construction workers, or a variety of other people. Play with the train sets and climb on the multi-level play set. The areas within Otterville are set up with parents in mind, too. The open floor plan and low dividing walls allow you see many areas at one time so it's easy to keep track of your roaming children.

For lunch, Totter's Otterville carries food that is baked, not fried, and peanut products are not allowed in the building. Applesauce, yogurt, pizza, hot dogs, and other kid favorites are available. They also serve salads, wraps, quesadillas, and sub sandwiches.

TRAMMEL FOSSIL PARK

Address: Tramway Drive, Sharonville, OH 45241

Website: www.sharonville.org/fossilpark.aspx

Hours: Daylight hours

Cost: Free

Ages: 3 and up

Stroller and wheelchair friendly: No

Length of visit: 1–2 hours

Description and comments:

Trammel Fossil Park is located in the midst of an industrial park in Sharonville. This 10-acre piece of property has avoided development. Here you can investigate the exposed earth and hunt for fossils. No special tools are required; most of the fossils are loose rocks that you will find right below your feet. There are signs explaining the theories of what happened on this land throughout history. Climb to the top and take in a bird's eye view looking south towards Cincinnati. Be sure to wear sturdy shoes for climbing on the hillside. Kids who are interested in fossils will love this place! Please note that there are portable toilets available during the summer months, but no running water on the premises. You are permitted to bring a representative sample of fossils home with you.

TRI-STATE WARBIRD MUSEUM

Address: 4021 Borman Drive, Batavia, OH 45103

Phone: (513) 735-4500

Website: www.tri-statewarbirdmuseum.org

Hours: Wednesday: 4 p.m.–7 p.m.
            Saturday: 10 a.m.–3 p.m.

Cost: $12 Adults
            $7 Students
            $7 Veterans
            Free to veterans in uniform and WWII veterans

Ages: 8 and up

Stroller and wheelchair friendly: Yes

Length of visit: 1–2 hours

Description and comments:

This 20,000 square foot facility houses over ten aircraft. Six of these aircraft are operational. The Warbird Museum stresses the importance of preserving the stories of a world at war and of honoring the people who have served our country. A display of historical artifacts relates to the history of the museum's aircraft. When you arrive, ask to see the film explaining the history of these airplanes. The museum also has a replica of WWII barracks and other items commemorating the efforts made by soldiers in this war.

The aircraft are stored in a hangar where planes are being restored. See the beautifully painted warbirds together in one place. These restored and operational planes — including the Cincinnati Miss and Tweety — are occasionally flown by their owners. Be careful with small kids because tripping hazards may exist on the hangar floor. Check the website for more information on the planes in their collection and pictures and video of the planes in action.

WARREN COUNTY HISTORY CENTER
AND GLENDOWER

Address: Warren County History Center:
105 South Broadway / Ohio Route 48, Lebanon,
OH 45036

Glendower Mansion:
105 Cincinnati Avenue, Lebanon, OH 45036

Phone: (513) 932-1817

Website: www.wchsmuseum.org

Hours: Museum
Tuesday–Saturday: 10 a.m.–4 p.m.
Closed holidays

Glendower Mansion
Seasonal. See website for details.

Cost: Museum only
$5 Adults
$3.50 Children (5–18)
$4.50 Seniors (65+)
$15 for a family with up to four children

Museum and Glendower Mansion
$8 Adults
$5 Children (5–18)
$7 Seniors (65+)
$28 for a family with up to four children

Ages: 4 and up

Stroller and wheelchair friendly: Yes

Length of visit: 1–2 hours

Description and comments:

The Warren County History Center's main exhibit area, Harmon Hall, houses a vast collection of items dating from prehistoric days to the early 1900s. There are three floors all containing different themes and items. The museum is expertly detailed and interesting for both parents and kids. A few favorite displays are the pioneer era collection of farming equipment, tools, and other items the pioneers used, including a sausage stuffer. On the main floor of the museum is the Village Green. This display is worthy of a much larger museum. The floor is lined with small storefronts featuring a toy store, drug store, post office, and many more. Inside each store front are many everyday objects from the early days of life in Warren County and Southern Ohio. You'll see kitchen utensils, cameras, clothing, toys, eyeglasses, medicines, etc. Have your kids try to imagine what life would have been like without cell phones, computers, and TVs.

Other treasures inside this museum are The Butterworth Cabin, which was once an Underground Railroad stop and an old country school complete with McGuffey readers. A large display on transportation shows carriages, sleighs, and even a 1908 Buick.

There are old Native American artifacts, artwork by Warren County Quaker artist Marcus Mote, and other works. Make your way to the second floor and you'll see the rooftops of the Village Green holding several exhibits. Musical instruments, furniture, art work, pottery, dishware, Bibles, and many more items are displayed here.

The Spirit of Tom Corwin Trail guides you through the museum explaining how Warren County's most famous citizen was involved in the history of the area. There are ten stations, each including a timeline and a description of

Tom's involvement in the area.

Glendower Mansion, located just a few blocks from the museum, offers tours with costumed interpreters. Glendower is a Northern Antebellum Greek Revival period home. It is shown as it would have been from 1845–1865. The home is located on five pristine acres with grounds suitable for tossing your blanket down and enjoying a picnic. Inside the home you'll see the period furnishings along with the history of the county. Glendower is not wheelchair or stroller accessible. See website for operating schedule.

DAYTON

ATTRACTIONS

1. Boonshoft Museum of Discovery
2. Carillon Historical Park
3. Carriage Hill MetroPark
4. Clifton George State Nature Preserve
5. Clifton Mill
6. The Dayton Art Institute
7. Dayton Aviation Heritage National Historic Park - Huffman Prairie Flying Field Interpretive Center
8. Dayton Aviation Heritage National Historic Park - Wright Cycle Company Complex
9. National Museum of the United States Air Force
10. SunWatch Indian Village/Archaeological Park
11. Wegerzyn Gardens MetroPark
12. Young's Jersey Dairy

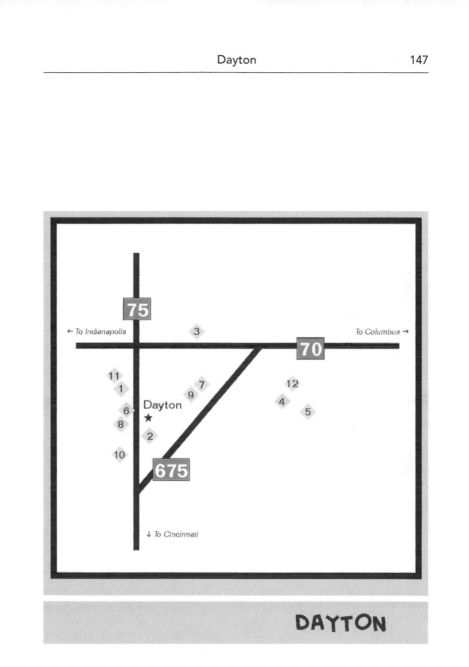

DAYTON

BOONSHOFT MUSEUM OF DISCOVERY

Address: 2600 DeWeese Parkway, Dayton, OH 45414

Phone: (937) 275-7431

Website: www.boonshoftmuseum.org

Hours: Monday–Saturday: 9 a.m.–5 p.m.
            Sunday: Noon–5 p.m.
            Closed some holidays

Cost: $8.50 Adults
            $7.50 Children (2–12)
            Free Children 1 and under
            $7.50 Seniors
            Free with Cincinnati Museum Center
            Membership

Ages: All ages

Stroller and wheelchair friendly: Yes

Length of visit: 2 hours–all day

Description and comments:

Boonshoft Museum of Discovery has a little bit of everything for kids of all ages. Younger children enjoy That Kids Playce, where they can dig in a pit of rubber shavings for dinosaur "bones," build with blocks, climb up the Tree House and slide back down. There are replicas of a SunWatch Thatched Hut, Pioneer Cabin, and Paul Lawrence Dunbar House. The Baby Garden is designed especially for children under 2. Older children love the three-story Climbing Tower and Slide. In Oscar Boonshoft Science Central, kids learn principles of science firsthand playing with an air blower, water table, and construction area. Kids can watch cool science experiments in the Science Theater and conduct experiments themselves in the Do Lab. See a show in the Space Theater for an additional $1 for regular planetarium shows or $3 for laser and special effects shows.

On the second floor, visitors discover more about wildlife and natural history. At the Tidal Pool, reach down and touch starfish, sea anemones, and sea cucumbers. One of our favorite places is the Discovery Zoo, with over one hundred animals and insects, completely indoors. Children and adults are enthralled with the playful river otters. Kids learn through pretend play in themed areas such as a landfill and recycling center, woodlands, an animal hospital, a courthouse, and a garage. Older children should investigate the exhibits on the Sonoran Desert, Glowing Geology, and the African Room. Amateur bird watchers love to wander out to the Tree House.

Make sure you get a daily schedule when you arrive so that you can plan your day around the shows and activities that interest you. There is a snack area with vending machines, but no restaurant. This museum has a reciprocal agreement with the Cincinnati Museum Center, making it free for Cincinnati Museum Center members. With such a diverse set of exhibits, there is surely something that will fascinate every member of your family. It is definitely worth the drive to Dayton.

CARILLON HISTORICAL PARK

Address: 1000 Carillon Boulevard, Dayton, OH 45409

Phone: (937) 293-2841

Website: www.daytonhistory.org

Hours: Monday–Saturday: 9:30 a.m.–5 p.m.
Sunday: Noon–5 p.m.
Closed some holidays

Cost: $8 Adults
$5 Children (3–17)
Free Children 2 and under
$7 Seniors

Check for AAA Discount

Ages: 3 and up

Stroller and wheelchair friendly: Yes

Length of visit: 3–6 hours

Description and comments:

Carillon Historical Park celebrates Dayton's rich history of invention. Set up like a village, it consists of over 25 historic buildings with various exhibits. The park is named for the 151-foot-tall Deeds Carillon. A carillon is a bell tower consisting of at least 23 bells. Deeds Carillon has 57 bells and is Ohio's largest. Concerts are performed every Sunday at 3 p.m. from May to October.

The most significant exhibit is the original 1905 Wright Flyer III, the world's first practical airplane, which is also a National Historic Landmark. On October 5, 1905, Wilbur flew 24 miles in 39 minutes 23 seconds, longer than the total duration of all the flights of 1903 and 1904. Other Wright Brothers exhibits include a replica of the Wright Brothers' Cycle Shop and family artifacts.

Other inventions displayed in the park include the cash register and automobile self-starter. Transportation exhibits show the evolution of transportation with displays of a Conestoga wagon, bicycles, early automobiles, an original lock of the Miami and Erie Canal, a trolley car, and locomotives. The park is also a great place to learn about the lifestyles of early Dayton residents. You can tour historic homes, a gristmill, a covered bridge, early gas station, print shop, tavern, and a one-room schoolhouse. The park includes a café, as well as picnic facilities, where you can have lunch. Carillon Historical Park provides a great opportunity to see a lot of history in one location.

CARRIAGE HILL METROPARK

Address: 7800 E. Shull Road, Dayton, OH 45424

Phone: (937) 278-2609

Website: www.metroparks.org/Parks/CarriageHill/
Home.aspx

Hours: Monday–Saturday: 10 a.m.–5 p.m.
Sunday: Noon–5 p.m.
Closed some holidays

Cost: Free

Ages: All ages

Stroller and wheelchair friendly: Gravel or grass paths,
large-wheeled strollers are best

Length of visit: 1–4 hours

Description and comments:

    Immerse yourself in 1880's farm life at Carriage Hill
Farm. The farm setting includes reconstructed and historical
buildings including a blacksmith shop, woodshop, historic
house, and barn. Park workers dress in period clothes and
present historical talks and demonstrations from 10 a.m.–
Noon and 1–4 p.m. each day. Demonstrations might include
churning butter, cooking, or horses pulling plows. Kids like
the demonstrations and petting the farm animals. Visiting
Carriage Hill gives you the feeling that you are actually
living on a farm in 1880. On the third Saturday of each month
from 8:30–9:15 a.m., Carriage Hill has a program in which
participants can help the farmer with chores like feeding the
animals and collecting eggs. Preregistration is required for
this program. A visitor's center contains additional exhibits

on the history of the area and a children's interactive center. There are several hiking and bridle trails for exploring the beautiful park grounds that include woodland and meadow areas, a fishing lake, and marsh. One short hike takes you to an old cemetery. There is an old-fashioned country store that sells candy by the piece. Be sure to stop there for an inexpensive treat for the kids. Picnic tables are available right outside the store. Consider packing your lunch if you visit on a weekday since the snack bar is not always open.

CLIFTON GORGE STATE NATURE PRESERVE

Address: 2331 State Route 343, Yellow Springs, OH 45387

Phone: (614) 265-6453

Website: www.ohiodnr.com/location/dnap/clifton/
tabid/882/Default.aspx

Hours: Daylight hours

Cost: Free

Ages: 3 and up

Stroller and wheelchair friendly: No

Length of visit: 1–3 hours

Description and comments:

Just west of Clifton Mill sits Clifton Gorge State Nature Preserve. This park has been called one of the nation's 50 Most Beautiful Places by National Geographic. This picturesque park has trails along the Little Miami River. This river had the honor of being named a National Scenic River in 1973. Many different trails are available to choose from, most overlooking the river far below in the deep gorge. Be careful to watch your kids near the steep cliffs and wear good walking shoes. The Narrows Trail is a perfect place to begin. It's a one-mile trail with some breathtaking views of the park. Many overlooks allow you to marvel at the beauty of the gorge. One interesting overlook explains the story of Darnell's Leap. The legend explains that Darnell was a member of Daniel Boone's team who was captured by Indians. He escaped into the woods but was pursued by his captors. At the narrow part of the gorge, Darnell miraculously leaped across the gorge and avoided being recaptured.

Follow the map and watch the signs while walking the trails. Gaze at waterfalls and maybe spot some wildlife. Your hike could range from one to six miles round trip. The Narrows Trail is fairly level terrain with no steep climbs. Other trails are longer and more challenging. The trails are not paved and are not stroller friendly. Be sure to bring your camera because you will want to remember the beauty of this hike.

CLIFTON MILL

Address: 75 Water Street, Clifton, OH 45316

Phone: (937) 767-5501

Website: www.cliftonmill.com

Hours: Monday–Friday: 9 a.m.–2:30 p.m.
Saturday and Sunday: 8 a.m.–2:30 p.m.
Closed some holidays

Cost: Restaurant meals range from $3.99 to $8.99

Tour (Available Sundays)
$3 Adults and Children

Christmas Lights
Day after Thanksgiving–January 1
$10 Adults and children 7 and up
Free Children 6 and under
Free Parking

Ages: 5 and up

Stroller and wheelchair friendly: Yes

Length of visit: Tour lasts about 20 minutes

Description and comments:

     Clifton Mill is one of the largest water powered grist mills still in existence. It remains as the only survivor of seven mills originally in the area. A visit to this mill will let you experience a slice of Ohio history. Tour the first floor and see the inner workings of the mill. Touch the giant grindstones and hear the water rushing under your feet providing the power for the mill. The miller describes the basic procedure for grinding wheat and corn and explains the history of the mill and the town. You will learn how life was different in this area before the Industrial Revolution.

The walls of the mill are decorated with over 300 antique flour bags. Some of these bright and colorful bags are over 100 years old and were used as advertising for mills across the country.

On site is a gift shop and restaurant. In the gift shop you can purchase whole wheat bread flour, cornmeal, and pancake mix. They carry delicious varieties of pancake mix like Apple Cinnamon, Buckwheat, Whole Wheat, and Blueberry. Take some home and let everyone help make breakfast. The restaurant serves pancakes, sandwiches, salads and soups. The kids might have trouble deciding between the numerous pancake choices! The menu is reasonably priced and the food is great.

On the grounds is a 90-foot authentic wooden covered bridge that crosses the Little Miami River. From the bridge you have attractive views of the Mill, Clifton Gorge, and the river and its waterfalls. Don't forget your camera! Next door is a 1940s gas station with memorabilia, old signs, and original products.

Christmas at Clifton Mill is spectacular, too! The entire area including the mill and waterfall are decorated with 3.5 million lights. Yes, you read that right, 3.5 million lights. Be there at 6 p.m. when the lights are turned on and see the area illuminated. They spend three months putting up the lights for a stunning show. See a collection of Santas, a huge outdoor miniature village, and a synchronized light and music show. This is worth the drive!

Within walking distance of the Mill are the Clifton Opera House, The Clifton Historical Society Museum, The Fish Decoy Company and Weber's Antique Mall. Make sure you also walk to Clifton Gorge State Nature Preserve (see previous listing).

Check the Clifton Mill website for a diagram, pictures, and explanations of how the mill works.

THE DAYTON ART INSTITUTE

Address: 456 Belmonte Park North, Dayton, OH 45405

Phone: (937) 223-5277

Website: www.daytonartinstitute.org

Hours: Wednesday, Friday, Saturday: 10 a.m. –5 p.m.
           Thursday: 10 a.m.–8 p.m.
           Sunday: Noon–5 p.m.
           Closed some holidays

Cost: $8 Adults (suggested donation)
           Free Children (17 and under)
           $5 Seniors (60+) (suggested donation)
           Some special exhibitions may have different fee

Ages: 3 and up

Stroller and wheelchair friendly: Yes

Length of visit: 1–5 hours

Description and comments:

The Dayton Art Institute is a great place to introduce your kids to fine art. It has an area just for kids called the Experiencenter, located in the lower rotunda, which is open the same hours as the rest of the museum. It contains two rotating exhibitions so there is something new every six months. These exhibitions always include real art, displayed at kids' eye level safely behind clear plastic, paired with hands-on educational activities. Their goal is for kids to look at the art and then complete the activity. They try to have something for all ages to enjoy, since visitors include toddlers as well as grandparents, but most activities are geared for the 8 to 12-year-old crowd. It might be challenging for kids to enjoy the galleries after the Experiencenter, so we recommend starting in the galleries and when the kids start getting restless, move on to the Experiencenter.

The museum gallery collections include ancient art, Native American art, glass, textiles, and various other pieces from all parts of the world. As we were touring, we had our children choose their favorite piece in each room and tell us why they liked it. This engaged them in the art and compelled them to think about it, and, as a result, they explored the galleries for far longer than we anticipated. The art institute also offers Gallery Hunts which consist of a checklist of items to find. These are available at the front desk or in the Experiencenter. Another popular program is the Kids Club, which is free, but requires registration. Your child will receive a Gallery Hunt and once they have completed four gallery hunts, they will receive a free art kit.

DAYTON AVIATION HERITAGE NATIONAL HISTORICAL PARK

Address: Wright Cycle Company Complex
            16 S. Williams Street, Dayton, OH 45402

            Huffman Prairie Flying Field Interpretive Center
            2380 Memorial Road, Wright-Patterson Air
            Force Base, Dayton, OH 45433

Phone: Wright Cycle Company Complex
            (937) 225-7705

            Huffman Prairie Flying Field Interpretive Center
            (937) 425-0008

Website: www.nps.gov/daav

Hours: Wright Cycle Company Complex
            Daily: 8:30 a.m.–5 p.m.
            Closed some holidays

            Huffman Prairie Flying Field Interpretive Center
            Daily: 8:30 a.m.–5 p.m.
            Memorial Day to Labor Day: 8:30 a.m.–6 p.m.
            Closed some holidays

Cost: Free

Ages: 4 and up

Stroller and wheelchair friendly: Yes

Length of visit: 2–4 hours

Description and comments:

Dayton is the "Birthplace of Aviation," and this national park provides a fantastic opportunity for your kids to learn about the Wright brothers and their quest to build a flying machine. The Wright Cycle Company Complex includes the Wright Cycle Company building, the Wright-Dunbar Interpretive Center, and the Aviation Trail Visitor Center and Museum. At the Wright-Dunbar Interpretive Center, learn about Wilbur and Orville Wright, as well as Paul Laurence Dunbar, an internationally-acclaimed African-American writer. Watch a film about the Wright brothers and explore interactive exhibits about their early careers in printing and bicycles, and their trials and errors in the process of inventing the airplane. Be sure to visit the Wright brothers' print shop and one of their bicycle shops, located adjacent to the interpretive center.

The Huffman Prairie Flying Field Interpretive Center is located near the field where the brothers performed their flying experiments. This center tells the continuing story of the Wright Brothers after their success at Kitty Hawk and has exhibits about the advancement of aviation. A favorite exhibit is the flight simulator where you take a turn maneuvering the Wright Flyer III. The film about the Wright brothers is also shown in this center.

Both interpretive centers offer a Junior Ranger program. Ask for the free booklet that contains activities for your child to complete. Upon completion, they present it to a ranger, receive a certificate and pin, and are sworn in as a Junior Ranger. Each site has different activities in the booklet and a different pin, so your child can receive pins from both locations.

Please note that your GPS unit may not correctly direct you to this park. Make sure to print out directions before you leave.

NATIONAL MUSEUM OF THE
UNITED STATES AIR FORCE

Address: 1100 Spaatz Street, Dayton, OH 45433

Phone: (937) 255-3286
           (937) 253-IMAX (for IMAX movie information)

Website: www.nationalmuseum.af.mil

Hours: Daily: 9 a.m.–5 p.m.
           Closed some holidays

Cost: Free admission to museum

           IMAX movie
           $6.75 Adults
           $5.75 Students (8–college)
           $4 Children (2–7)
           $6 Seniors

Ages: 3 and up

Stroller and wheelchair friendly: Yes

Length of visit: 2–4 hours

Description and comments:

The Air Force Museum is a must-see for anyone who is even mildly interested in aviation and the history of aviation. There is so much to see and learn that you will easily enjoy this amazing museum. Wear your walking shoes to see over 17 acres of exhibits. Your visit begins with the Wright Brothers and early attempts at aviation, continuing chronologically through to the stealth fighters.

This is the world's largest and oldest military aviation museum. It contains over 300 aircraft and aerospace vehicles, thousands of historical items, and many interactive exhibits. You'll learn about the history of flight and how it became the precision technology of today.

You will be in awe of the massive size of some of these aircraft. Crane your neck to take in the towering Intercontinental Ballistic Missiles. Walk through four Presidential aircraft including the Boeing 707 which carried the body of President Kennedy. You will understand the role of aviation in the defense of our country.

The museum contains an IMAX movie theater and a Morphis Movie Ride. (Separate charge for each attraction.) IMAX shows start on the hour. The Morphis is a flight simulator that seats 14 people. Several museum tours are offered daily. Make sure you preregister if you are interested in these free tours. Check the website for more information. A souvenir shop, book store, and cafeteria are also available.

On the third Saturday of each month, the museum hosts a Family Day from 10 a.m. to 3 p.m. Each Family Day has a different theme and offers hands-on activities and demonstrations. All of the activities are free. Check the website for the schedule and themes.

SUNWATCH INDIAN VILLAGE / ARCHAEOLOGICAL PARK

Address: 2301 W. River Road, Dayton, OH 45418

Phone: (937) 268-8199

Website: www.sunwatch.org

Hours: Tuesday–Saturday: 9 a.m.–5 p.m.
Sunday: Noon–5 p.m.
Closed some holidays

Cost: $5 Adults
$3 Children (6–17)
Free Children 5 and under
$3 Seniors (60+)

Ages: 3 and up

Stroller and wheelchair friendly: Yes

Length of visit: 2 hours

Description and comments:

SunWatch Village is a National Historic Landmark and the original site of an 800-year-old Native American village. Begin your visit inside with a film explaining more about the village and its history. The interpretive center also holds exhibits to explain the lifestyle of the Fort Ancient Native American culture. Learn about the food they grew in their garden and how they stored it. See how their houses were set up. Next, venture outside to experience life in the village. Excavations took place from 1971 to 1988 and revealed a planned settlement. SunWatch has now partly reconstructed the village. Walk the circle path and see homes, meeting places, and other structures. The buildings feature realistic props like animal skins on the small beds and vegetables ready to be cooked over the fire. Many signs around the park explain the purposes of each structure and everyone is encouraged to ask questions. Kids will have a better understanding of prehistoric Native American culture after their visit to SunWatch.

WEGERZYN GARDENS METROPARK

Address: 1301 E. Siebenthaler Avenue, Dayton, OH
45414

Phone: (937) 277-6545

Website: www.metroparks.org/Parks/WegerzynGarden

Hours: Park Grounds
April–October
Daily: 8 a.m.–10 p.m.
November–March
Daily: 8 a.m.–8 p.m.

Closed Christmas and New Year's Day

Children's Discovery Garden
June–August
Daily: 10 a.m.–8 p.m.
April, May, September, October
Daily: 10 a.m.–6 p.m.
November–March
Daily: 10 a.m.–4 p.m.

Cost: Free

Ages: All ages
Children's Discovery Garden is designed for
ages 3–11.

Stroller and wheelchair friendly: Yes

Length of visit: 2–4 hours

Description and comments:

Wegerzyn Gardens is a delightful gem in Dayton worth discovering. Start your visit at the Children's Discovery

Garden, where kids learn and play at the same time. The garden mimics the different habitat areas found in Ohio including woods, prairie, wetlands, and a cave. Each of these areas has interactive features for kids. They can dig, build a fairy house, look for fossils in a cave, and peek at roots through a root window. They can also pump water into a watering can and water the plants in the garden. Other features include a sand play table, music maze, and playhouse. Be sure to pack a swimsuit, sunscreen, and towel, so your kids can shower themselves under the waterfall.

On weekdays from Memorial Day through Labor Day, Wegerzyn offers a special kids' activity at 2 p.m. that lasts 30–45 minutes. It is different each day and could include feeding the fish, story time, games, or an adventure walk.

Spend some time exploring the rest of the park. Stroll through beautiful formal gardens and follow the boardwalk trail through a swamp garden. There is also a nature trail for those who want to hike. Pack a lunch to enjoy at the picnic facilities.

YOUNG'S JERSEY DAIRY

Address: 6880 Springfield-Xenia Road, Yellow Springs,
OH 45387

Phone: (937) 325-0629

Website: www.youngsdairy.com

Hours: Restaurant Summer Hours
Monday–Friday: 11 a.m.–9 p.m.
Saturday and Sunday: 8 a.m.–9 p.m.
Call or check website for seasonal hours

Petting Zoo
April–October: 10 a.m.–10 p.m.
November–March: 10 a.m.–6 p.m.

Cost: 10 cents for goat food
$2 Moovers and Shakers train ride
$1.25 Giant slide ride
$5–$13 Bucket of golf balls
$4.50 Putt-putt golf

Ages: All ages

Stroller and wheelchair friendly: Yes

Length of visit: 4–5 hours

Description and comments:

Young's Jersey Dairy has a plethora of activities to
entertain you on your visit. Bring some change to purchase
feed for the animals in the petting zoo. It will set you back
10 cents for a small handful of specially formulated goat
feed with grains, vitamins and minerals to keep the goats
healthy. Kids are thrilled to have the goats nibble the feed
right from their hands. The cows and pigs are there too, but

not for feeding. Ride the new Moovers and Shakers train which runs during the summer and takes your kids on a trip around the farm. You'll keep everyone busy on the giant slide, two different miniature golf courses, a driving range, and batting cages.

Be sure to plan your trip to include a meal. Choose from two different restaurants. The Golden Jersey Inn has some great food available in a charming barn made with wooden pegs and wood plank siding. The kids' menu includes traditional favorites and also their yummy homemade chicken and dumplings. The grown-up menu also includes traditional favorites, a lighter section, salads, soups, and sandwiches, many with a unique spin. They are also vegetarian friendly. Make sure to save room for dessert, as Young's is famous for its ice cream desserts. The kids' meals include a scoop of ice cream, but you can request a coupon to redeem later at The Dairy Store, the other onsite restaurant. Check the website for complete menus and prices.

Young's hosts many special events on weekends throughout the summer and fall. Check the website for details. If you're interested in extending your day, John Bryan State Park is just a few miles away, as is the Little Miami Bike trail. Many Young's guests do their bicycling then reward themselves by indulging in a creamy treat!

COLUMBUS, LEXINGTON, LOUISVILLE AND INDIANAPOLIS

ATTRACTIONS

Columbus

1. Anthony-Thomas Chocolate Factory
2. Central Ohio Fire Museum & Learning Center
3. COSI
4. The Santa Maria
5. The Topiary Park

Lexington

6. American Saddlebred Museum
7. Kentucky Horse Park

Louisville

8. Louisville Slugger Museum & Factory

Indianapolis

9. The Children's Museum of Indianapolis

See Cincinnati & Dayton Maps for Respective Attractions.

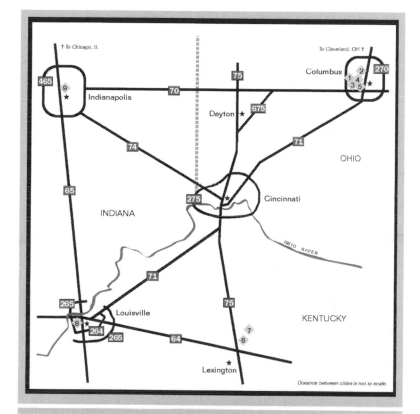

COLUMBUS, LEXINGTON, LOUISVILLE, AND INDIANAPOLIS

MILEAGE	
Cincinnati to Columbus	100 miles
Cincinnati to Dayton	50 miles
Cincinnati to Indianapolis	115 miles
Cincinnati to Lexington	90 miles
Cincinnati to Louisville	105 miles

COLUMBUS

ANTHONY-THOMAS CHOCOLATE FACTORY

__Address:__   1777 Arlingate Lane, Columbus, OH, 43228

__Phone:__   (614) 274-8405
(877) 226-3921

__Website:__   www.anthony-thomas.com

__Hours:__   Tuesday & Thursday: 9:30 a.m.–2:30 p.m. for tours (no reservation necessary)

Monday–Thursday: 9:30 a.m.–2:30 p.m. for groups of 10 or more by appointment only

__Cost:__   Free

__Ages:__   3 and up

__Stroller and wheelchair friendly:__ Yes

__Length of visit:__ 1 hour (allow extra time to shop in the gift shop)

__Description and comments:__

If you love chocolate be sure to visit Anthony-Thomas Chocolate Factory. Take part in a guided tour of the chocolate factory from a catwalk overlooking the production floor. The Anthony-Thomas factory makes over 25,000 pounds of chocolates each shift. Gaze at the huge copper kettles and the silver wrapped pipes containing liquid chocolate. The tour guide explains each step of the chocolate making process from harvesting the beans to the packaging of delicious candy. At the end of the tour enjoy a complimentary buckeye candy or a crème filled chocolate. Help your children understand that these treats originate somewhere other than the grocery store. We were told that the employees are allowed to have as much chocolate as they want to eat. We didn't see anyone taste any, but maybe you will!

CENTRAL OHIO FIRE MUSEUM & LEARNING CENTER

Address: 260 N. Fourth Street, Columbus, OH 43215

Phone: (614) 464-4099

Website: www.centralohiofiremuseum.com

Hours: Tuesday–Saturday: 10 a.m.–4 p.m.

Cost: $6 Adults
            $4 Children
            $5 Seniors
            Call ahead for group tours and rates

Ages: 3 and up

Stroller and wheelchair friendly: Yes

Length of visit: 1–2 hours

Description and comments:

The Central Ohio Fire Museum is housed in a restored fire station originally built in 1908. Several "man-powered" and "horse-powered" fire trucks are on display. In the early days of the firehouse, the horses lived in the station with the firefighters and you can step through the original stalls that housed them. The stall doors have dents remaining from the horses' hooves. A guide leads you through the museum, explaining the equipment and the history of firefighting and of the station. You will hear the ringing bell that signals a fire. The museum also contains a children's play area complete with a working fire truck cab. Push the buttons and hear the sirens roar. Slide down a fire pole and try on junior sized fire gear.

The back of the museum contains a very thorough fire

education center. Your children will practice making a 911 call and witness the devastating results of a fire. One room displays items that have been burned in real fires. Learn about safety in your home and understand the effects of several types of kitchen fires. You will be convinced of the importance of fire safety by visiting a bedroom that has been destroyed by a house fire. After your tour, little firefighters receive a memento to remind them of their visit.

COSI

Address: 333 W. Broad Street, Columbus, OH 43215

Phone: (614) 228-2674
          (888) 819-2674

Website: www.cosi.org

Hours: Wednesday–Saturday: 10 a.m.–5 p.m.
          Sunday: Noon–6 p.m.
          Last Friday of Every Month: 5–9 p.m.

          Closed some holidays. Closed part of
          September for maintenance. Check website
          for schedule.

Cost: Exhibits and Live Shows:
          $14.25 Adults (13–59)
          $9.25 Children (2–12)
          $13.25 Seniors (60+)

          Extreme Screen Movie Theater:
          $7.50 Each film, all ages

          Value Pass (Exhibits, Live Shows, and Movies):
          $20.25 Adults (13–59)
          $15.25 Children (2–12)
          $19.25 Seniors (60+)
          $4 Parking

          Exhibits and live shows are free with
          Cincinnati Museum Center membership.
          Movie tickets require purchase.

Ages: All ages

Stroller and wheelchair friendly: Yes

Length of visit: 2 hours–all day

Description and comments:

COSI is a science museum that will appeal to everyone in the family. The acronym stands for Center of Science and Industry, but everyone calls it COSI. The excitement begins as soon as you enter the building. Look above to see a unicycle on a high wire that older kids and adults may want to ride later in your visit. Also in the lobby is the electrostatic generator show where you learn about electricity and see someone's hair stand up straight! When you purchase your admission, be sure to get a show schedule so that you can plan your day around the shows you want to see. One of our favorites is Rat Basketball, where you can watch two rats compete against each other putting a ball through a basket. You'll learn about how rats are trained. Also very popular are the shows on the Gadgets Stage. These shows vary seasonally and may include chemistry, dry ice, or explosions.

Exhibits are organized into about ten different areas within the museum. Parents with infants, toddlers, or preschoolers will want to spend some time in Little Kidspace, which was designed for and is restricted to young children. Kids can build with blocks, climb and slide, pretend to drive an ambulance, and play in the water area. Older siblings can spend time in the Hang Out room, which has activities especially for them and is monitored so that parents can spend time with the younger children.

Children of all ages are fascinated with learning about the properties of water in the Ocean area. They can balance a ball on a fountain of water and make some waves. They will also have fun exploring the submarine area. The Gadgets exhibit area is another fun place with activities like pulling your own weight with ropes and pulleys, and redirecting a laser beam using mirrors. In the Gadgets Café you can take apart everyday objects to see how they work or do science experiments. Reservations are required; sign up early in the day.

School-age children will enjoy the Space exhibit where they can maneuver a robotic Mars rover, learn about gravity, and engage in interactive computer activities. In the Life exhibit area, kids can learn about gestation, birthing, and aging. A new laboratory opened in 2009 that allows visitors to watch actual research studies on physical activity and nutrition. The Progress exhibit is a place to learn about the history of innovation with displays on Morse code, the evolution of electricity, and early televisions.

Big Science Park is an outdoor area where you can ride a rotor ride and use a giant lever to lift a car. WOSU is a working TV & radio studio. There are also many interesting hallway exhibits. One of our favorites is the hot air balloon area. The Extreme Screen is a movie theater with a screen that is 83 feet wide and 7 stories tall. There are two movies shown that alternate every hour. There is an additional fee required for the films.

COSI's website has helpful information including suggested itineraries for different ages, and suggested activities in each exhibit area. The museum has a gift shop as well as a restaurant onsite which is a convenient option for lunch. You are also allowed to carry in a packed lunch and eat in the lunch room. COSI is a great museum and well worth the drive to Columbus. It has a reciprocal agreement with the Cincinnati Museum Center, making it free for Cincinnati Museum Center members.

THE SANTA MARIA

Address: 25 Marconi Boulevard, Columbus, OH 43215

Phone: (614) 645-8760

Website: www.santamaria.org

Hours: Spring
Wednesday–Friday: 10 a.m.–3 p.m.
Saturday and Sunday: Noon–5 p.m.

Summer
Wednesday–Friday: 10 a.m.–5 p.m.
Saturday and Sunday: Noon–6 p.m.

Fall
Wednesday–Friday: 10 a.m.–3 p.m.
Saturday and Sunday: Noon–5 p.m.

Closed some holidays

Cost: $4 Adults
$2.50 Children (5–17)
$3.50 Seniors

Ages: 3 and up

Stroller and wheelchair friendly: Strollers not permitted, but can be parked at visitor's center. Wheelchair accessible on main deck only.

Length of visit: 1 hour

Description and comments:

Go back in time as you step aboard The Santa Maria, a replica of Christopher Columbus' flagship, in downtown Columbus. The Santa Maria floats in the Scioto River at Battelle Riverfront Park, and was opened in 1992 to commemorate the 500-year anniversary of the discovery of America by the city's namesake, Christopher Columbus. During a 45-minute tour, you learn how the ship was built, about life aboard the ship, and how its voyage changed the world. Descend into the hold to see where the supplies were stored and learn how they outsmarted stowaway mice. You also learn what the sailors wore, what they ate, how they cooked, and some of the nautical terminology they used. See the sleeping quarters of Christopher Columbus and compare them to the sleeping quarters of the crew. Find out how the ship was navigated, see the tools and learn the methods used to draw the maps during their journey, and learn how the sailors could defend the ship from attack. During the summer months, costumed volunteers are on board helping with the tours and acting as the crew. Older kids will have learned about The Santa Maria in school and will appreciate it in a whole new way after exploring the ship themselves.

Batelle Riverfront Park has walking/biking trails, picnic tables, and the Columbus Fire Department Memorial, housing a bell and an eternal flame. Also in the park is the Pickaweekee Children's Fountain. This fountain contains several bronze animal statues all featured in the mythical story of Pickaweekee. You can read the story about Pickaweekee and the various animals he meets on a plaque near the fountain.

There are several metered parking spots on Marconi Boulevard, directly in front of The Santa Maria.

THE TOPIARY PARK

Address: 480 E. Town Street, Columbus, OH 43215

Phone: (614) 645-0197

Website: www.topiarypark.org

Hours: Park Grounds:
Daylight hours, year round
Best viewing: April–November

Visitor's Center:
April through Mid–November
Tuesday, Saturday, and Sunday: 11 a.m.–3 p.m.

Cost: Free

Ages: All

Stroller and wheelchair friendly: Yes

Length of visit: 1 hour

Description and comments:

The Topiary Park, in downtown Columbus, is perhaps the most unique attraction in this book. The theme of the garden is a famous post-impressionist painting by Georges Seurat, A Sunday on the Island of La Grande Jatte. This painting is well known for its use of pointillism. We applaud the creative mind that dreamed up the idea to recreate a painting using shrubbery. It is truly one of a kind. All of the figures in the painting have been recreated in topiary form, including 54 people, eight boats, three dogs, a monkey, and a cat. Kids get a kick out of seeing people and animals carved from shrubs. They can walk up to them, around them, and view them from all sides. Touching and climbing are not permitted. Even the river in the painting was recreated by installing a pond in the park. A bronze plaque on one of the paths marks the point where you stand to view the figures as they appear in the painting. The painting does not include a cat and it is not visible from the plaque, but was added to the park as a fun touch. Challenge your children to find it. For some additional fun, visit the website and look for the education packet. It includes an outline drawing of the painting that you can print and have your kids color. Other educational materials are also included. The park includes benches and picnic facilities. This is a delightful spot to have a picnic lunch after visiting another attraction in Columbus. The visitor's center is open seasonally on Tuesdays and weekends and includes a gift shop. Check the website for information on scheduling a docent-led tour of the park. Restrooms are open daily.

LEXINGTON

AMERICAN SADDLEBRED MUSEUM

Address: 4083 Iron Works Parkway, Lexington, KY 40511

Phone: (859) 259-2746

Website: www.americansaddlebredmuseum.org

Hours: Memorial Day–Labor Day
Daily: 9 a.m.–6 p.m.

September–May
Daily: 9 a.m.–5 p.m.

Closed on Mondays and Tuesdays,
November–March

Closed some holidays

Cost: Includes admission to the Kentucky Horse Park

March 15–October 31
$16 Adults
$8 Children (7–12)
Free Children 6 and under
$15 Seniors (65+)
$3 Parking

November 1–March 14
$9 Adults
$6 Children (7–12)
Free Children 6 and under
$8 Seniors (65+)
Free Parking

Ages: 3 and up

Stroller and wheelchair friendly: Yes

Length of visit: 1 hour

Description and comments:

Don't miss seeing the American Saddlebred Museum on your visit to the Kentucky Horse Park. The museum is located on the grounds of the Kentucky Horse Park and is included in the admission price. See award winning movies and learn about the role that the Saddlebred horse has played in the history of America. There are many interactive, one-of-a-kind displays for kids. It also houses a large library and a gift shop. This is a fun stop that pairs perfectly with the Kentucky Horse Park.

KENTUCKY HORSE PARK

Address: 4089 Iron Works Parkway, Lexington, KY 40511

Phone: (859) 233-4304
           (800) 678-8813

Website: www.kyhorsepark.com

Hours: March 15–October 31
           Daily: 9 a.m.–5 p.m.

           November 1–March 14
           Wednesday–Sunday: 9 a.m.–5 p.m.

Cost: Includes admission to the American
           Saddlebred Museum

           March 15–October 31
           $16 Adults
           $8 Children (7–12)
           Free Children 6 and under
           $15 Seniors (62+)
           $3 Parking

           November 1–March 14
           $9 Adults
           $6 Children (7–12)
           Free Children 6 and under
           $8 Seniors (62+)
           Free Parking

           There is an extra fee for pony rides, horseback
           rides and farm tours. Check the website for
           more information.

           Check for AAA discount.

Ages: 3 and up

Stroller and wheelchair friendly: Yes

Length of visit: 3–6 hours

Description and comments:

If you have a horse lover in your family, or if you are interested in the pastime that has made Kentucky famous, then the Kentucky Horse Park is worth the trip. This is a hands-on park and living museum. It is situated on a stunning campus in the rolling hills of Kentucky. Younger kids (under 90 pounds) can take a pony ride; while the older kids (at least 7 years old and 4 feet tall) may venture on a 45-minute trail ride (both for an additional fee). See a wide range of shows including the Parade of Breeds. In this program you will see some of the 29 breeds in the park and learn what makes each of them unique. The handlers are handsome in authentic clothing as would have been worn in different parts of the world. After the show there is time to visit the horses and talk to their handlers.

See a Mare and Foal show where the babies and moms are displayed together. Another performance will explain how to take care of a horse and give some audience members a chance to participate in some of these tasks.

See the Draft Horses being groomed and prepared for their day of work pulling the trolleys. Later take the free ten-minute narrated trolley ride highlighting the different areas of the park.

In the Hall of Champions, you will see many former award-winning race horses that now make their home at the Kentucky Horse Park. View clips of their races and snap some close up pictures as the horses are paraded past the audience. Notice the tombstones of the former stars of the park in the Legends of the Park. The burial place of the Legendary Man O' War is marked by a majestic bronze sculpture.

Next, venture indoors to the International Museum of the Horse. This museum "is committed to educating the general public, equestrian and academic communities about the relationship between man and the horse throughout history and the world." In its 38,000 square feet you will take a historical journey of the horse throughout time. Your kids will recognize many well known lessons straight from their history books in the displays. The Kentucky Horse Park also has two free movies explaining the relationships between horses and people. There is food available for purchase inside the park. If you pack a lunch, bring a blanket and enjoy a picnic on the grounds outside of the park.

LOUISVILLE

LOUISVILLE SLUGGER MUSEUM & FACTORY

Address: 800 West Main Street, Louisville, KY 40202

Phone: (877) 775-8443

Website: www.sluggermuseum.org

Hours: Monday–Saturday: 9 a.m.–5 p.m.
Sunday: Noon–5 p.m.
Check website for extended summer hours
and holiday closings

Cost: $10 Adults (13–59)
$5 Children (6–12)
Free Children 5 and under
$9 Seniors (60+)

There is an extra charge for the batting cages.
($1 for 20 balls)

Ages: 3 and up

Stroller and wheelchair friendly: Yes

Length of visit: 2 hours for museum visit; 25 minutes for factory tour

Description and comments:

You'll be certain you've found the Louisville Slugger Museum & Factory when you catch sight of The World's Biggest Bat leaning against the side of the building. This bat was constructed with the exact, scaled dimensions of Babe Ruth's bat. Inside the building is an oversized sculpture of a baseball glove. Take the stairs to the second floor and snap a picture of your kids in the monstrous mitt.

When you arrive, purchase your ticket for the museum

and factory tour. You will receive a ticket for the next available tour. While you are waiting for your tour to begin, run the bases of the field while listening to the sounds of famous plays being called. You can also practice your swing in Bud's Batting Cage. Check for the starting times of the movie The Heart of the Game and be sure to fit this into your schedule.

The tour takes you through the factory where the bats are produced. (Note the bat production schedule posted on the website. Bats are not produced on Sundays or holidays.) Smell the sawdust while watching the precision methods for crafting the bats to the exact specifications of each player. Talk to the employees at each step of production and see how these Louisville Slugger bats are made. At the end of the tour, each person will receive a miniature bat as a memento of their visit.

The museum was renovated in 2009 and added many displays. New exhibits include a display featuring a Babe Ruth bat. Babe carved a notch in this bat for each home run hit with it. There is a new interactive area with memorabilia of some of baseball's unforgettable moments. Also included is a hands-on display of bats used by professional ball players. A Joe DiMaggio bat (never before on display) is now available for visitors to see. There is also a children's activity area included in the museum.

In the gift shop you can order a personalized bat with either your name or your signature on it. They also carry Louisville Slugger walking canes and many other souvenirs.

The Louisville Slugger Museum is across the street from the Louisville Science Center, a fascinating museum which has a reciprocal agreement with the Cincinnati Museum Center, making it free for members.

INDIANAPOLIS

THE CHILDREN'S MUSEUM OF INDIANAPOLIS

Address: 3000 N. Meridian Street, Indianapolis, IN
46208

Phone: (317) 334-3322

Website: www.childrensmuseum.org

Hours: March–Labor Day
Daily: 10 a.m.–5 p.m.

Labor Day–February
Tuesday–Sunday: 10 a.m.–5 p.m.
Closed some holidays

Cost: $16.50 Adults
$11.50 Children (2–17)
Free Children 1 and under, with
accompanying adult
$15.50 Seniors (60+)

Occasional free days and evenings; check
website for details.

Free Parking in garage

The Children's Museum of Indianapolis does
not have a reciprocal agreement with
Cincinnati Museum Center.

Ages: All ages

Stroller and wheelchair friendly: Yes

Length of visit: 2–6 hours

Description and comments:

The Indianapolis Children's Museum houses an impressive collection of 11 major galleries exploring the physical and natural sciences, history, world cultures, and the arts. Dinosphere might be a favorite spot for junior paleontologists. Walk among the dinosaurs, dig up fossils, and listen to a thunderstorm roll in above you. A working turn-of-the-century carousel delights the young and the old alike. Climb aboard and experience the sights and sounds of the magical merry-go-round for an additional $1 fee. An 1868, 35-foot long steam engine is at the center of the All Aboard train exhibit. Guests can view both real and model trains in this area while exploring what life was like in the glory days of the locomotive. Playscape welcomes visitors ages five and younger (with their parents) where they can play, build, pretend, and splash. Walking up the ramp in the center of the building you can't miss the brilliant, 43-foot tall, Dale Chihuly glass sculpture, "Fireworks of Glass." This amazing centerpiece will fascinate children and adults of every age. One of the films in the Planetarium (included with admission) explains Chihuly's glass blowing process. Other exhibits in the museum include an Egyptian tomb, a hands-on science gallery, a biotechnology learning area, and Health House — a place where kids learn about making healthy choices. The museum's website includes more information on activities and galleries most suitable for each age group.

At the end of the day, gather at the top of the ramp for a parade. Each child will receive a flag to carry and they will march happily out of the museum. What a great way to end the day!

Part Three

PLANNING HELP

PLANNING YOUR OWN ADVENTURES

This section is designed to help you plan your own adventures. We have provided some sample itineraries to get you off to a quick start, for both summer and year-round schedules. Following the itineraries, our Attraction Table contains an alphabetical list of all the attractions in table format, clearly showing which activities fit into each category and location. Use this list to find adventures suitable for your family. Take special note of our free attractions to help you manage the cost of your adventures.

SAMPLE ITINERARIES:

Summer 1:
Sawyer Point and Serpentine Wall
Loveland Castle – Chateau LaRoche
Pyramid Hill Sculpture Park & Museum
SunWatch Indian Village / Archaeological Park
Cincinnati Nature Center – Rowe Woods
Parky's Farm at Winton Woods Park
Trammel Fossil Park
Cincinnati Reds Hall of Fame & Museum
Jungle Jim's International Market
Cincinnati Fire Museum

Summer 2:
Fort Ancient
BB Riverboats
Carillon Historical Park
Megaland at Colerain Park

William Howard Taft National Historic Site
Mariemont Bell Tower Carillon
River Downs
Carriage Hill MetroPark
Cincinnati Museum Center
Behringer Crawford Museum

Year-Round 1:

January - National Museum of the United States Air Force
February - CoCo Key Water Resort
March - The Dayton Art Institute or Cincinnati Art Museum
April - Carillon Historical Park
May - Pyramid Hill Sculpture Park & Museum
June - Carew Tower Observation Deck/Fountain Square
July - Fort Ancient
August - William Howard Taft National Historic Site
September - Wegerzyn Gardens MetroPark
October - Cincinnati Nature Center – Rowe Woods
November - Behringer Crawford Museum
December - Cincinnati History Museum at Cincinnati
        Museum Center

Year-Round 2:

January - Boonshoft Museum of Discovery
February - Cincinnati Fire Museum
March - UnMuseum at the Contemporary Arts Center
April - Sky Galley Restaurant at Lunken Airport/Lunken
        Airport Playfield
May - Warren County History Center
June - Trammel Fossil Park
July - Irons Fruit Farm
August - Dayton Aviation Heritage National Historical Park
September - Loveland Castle – Chateau LaRoche

October - The Santa Maria
November - Museum of Natural History and Science at
        Cincinnati Museum Center
December - Clifton Mill

Free	Gardens	History	Museums	Outdoor	Planes	Play Areas	Preschoolers	Tours	Trains	Transportation	Walking/Hiking	Central Cincinnati	Greater Cincinnati	Dayton	Columbus	Lexington	Louisville	Indianapolis
						x	x						x					
		x	x													x		
										x			x					
x								x							x			
				x				x		x		x						
				x		x	x						x					
		x	x				x		x	x			x					
x				x							x		x					
		x	x			x	x								x			
				x			x					x						
		x	x	x	x		x			x	x				x			
x		x		x		x	x				x			x				
		x	x				x	x								x		
		x	x			x	x		x									x
x		x	x	x			x			x			x					
•			x				•					x						
		x	x				x						x					
		x	x				x				x		x					
	x			x		x	x				x		x					
x					x			x		x			x					
		x	x										x					
	x			x			x						x					
x				x							x				x			
		x						x							x			
						x	x						x					
				x		x							x					

ATTRACTION	Page #	Animals	Archaeology	Art	Bells	Dinosaurs
COSI	179					
Creation Museum	89	x	x			x
Crooked Run Nature Preserve	91	x				
The Dayton Art Institute	159			x		
Dayton Aviation Heritage National Historical Park	161					
Duke Energy Children's Museum at Cincinnati Museum Center	38					
EnterTRAINment Junction	92					
Fort Ancient	94		x			
Fountain Square	41					
Garden of Hope	96		x			
Gorman Heritage Farm	98	x				
Grant Boyhood Home and Schoolhouse	100					
Heritage Village Museum at Sharon Woods Park	102					
Highfield Discovery Garden at Glenwood Gardens Park	104					
Irons Fruit Farm	107	x				
Jungle Jim's International Market	108					
Kentucky Horse Park	189	x				
Kings Island and Boomerang Bay Waterpark	110					x
Krohn Conservatory	43					
Lebanon Mason Monroe Railroad	113					
Little Miami Bike Trail	115					
Louisville Slugger Museum & Factory	193					
Loveland Castle – Chateau LaRoche	117					
Lunken Airport Playfield	45					
Mariemont Bell Tower Carillon	119				x	

Free	Gardens	History	Museums	Outdoor	Planes	Play Areas	Preschoolers	Tours	Trains	Transportation	Walking/Hiking	Central Cincinnati	Greater Cincinnati	Dayton	Columbus	Lexington	Louisville	Indianapolis
		X	X			X	X								X			
	X	X	X										X					
X				X								X	X					
•			X				X							X				
X		X	X		X					X				X				
			X			X	X				X							
		X	X			X	X		X	X			X					
		X	X	X				X			X		X					
•	X			X								X						
•	X			X				X					X					
	X	X		X			X				X		X					
		X											X					
		X	X	X		•	•	X					X					
	X			X		X	X		X				X					
				X			X						X					
								X					X					
		X	X													X		
				X		X	X						X					
•	X						X					X						
							X		X	X			X					
X				X							X		X					
		X	X					X									X	
	X	X		X									X					
				X		X	X				X	X						
X								X					X					

ATTRACTION	Page #	Animals	Archaeology	Art	Bells	Dinosaurs
Megaland at Colerain Park	121					
Metamora, Indiana	122					
Museum of Natural History and Science at Cincinnati Museum Center	46	x				x
National Museum of the United States Air Force	163					
National Underground Railroad Freedom Center	49					
Newport Aquarium	51	x				
Noah's Ark Farm & Petting Zoo	124	x				
Parky's Farm at Winton Woods Park	126	x				
Parky's Wet Playgrounds	128					
Purple People Bridge	53					
Pyramid Hill Sculpture Park & Museum	130			x		
Railway Museum of Greater Cincinnati	132					
Ride the Ducks - Newport	54					
River Downs	133					
Robert D. Lindner Family OMNIMAX Theater at Cincinnati Museum Center	56					
The Santa Maria	182					
Sawyer Point and Serpentine Wall	57					
Serpent Mound	135		x			
Sky Galley Restaurant at Lunken Airport	59					
Sunrock Farm	137	x				
SunWatch Indian Village / Archaeological Park	165		x			
The Topiary Park	184			x		
Totter's Otterville at Johnny's Toys	138					x
Trammel Fossil Park	140	x				
Tri-State Warbird Museum	141					
UnMuseum at the Contemporary Arts Center	60			x		

Free	Gardens	History	Museums	Outdoor	Planes	Play Areas	Preschoolers	Tours	Trains	Transportation	Walking/Hiking	Central Cincinnati	Greater Cincinnati	Dayton	Columbus	Lexington	Louisville	Indianapolis
				X		X	X				X		X					
		X		X						X	X		X					
		X	X			X	X					X						
X		X	X		X					X				X				
		X	X									X						
						X	X					X						
				X			X						X					
				X		X	X						X					
				X		X	X						X					
•				X						X	X	X						
	X		X	X							X		X					
		X	X	X					X	X			X					
		X		X			X	X		X		X						
X				X			X						X					
											X							
		X		X			X	X		X					X			
•				X		X	X					X	X					
•				X								X		X				
					X					X			X					
				X			X	X					X					
			X	X			X							X				
X	X			X													X	
				X		X	X		X				X					
X				X			X						X					
		X	X		X					X			X					
•			X				X					X						

ATTRACTION	Page #	Animals	Archaeology	Art	Bells	Dinosaurs
Verdin Bell and Clock Museum	62				x	
Warren County History Center and Glendower	143					
Wegerzyn Gardens MetroPark	167					
William Howard Taft National Historic Site	63					
World Peace Bell	65				x	
Young's Jersey Dairy	169	x				

- *See individual listings for parking fees, restricted days, and specific cost information.*

Free	Gardens	History	Museums	Outdoor	Planes	Play Areas	Preschoolers	Tours	Trains	Transportation	Walking/Hiking	Central Cincinnati	Greater Cincinnati	Dayton	Columbus	Lexington	Louisville	Indianapolis
		X	X					X				X						
		X	X											X				
X	X			X		X	X				X			X				
X		X						X				X						
X				X				X				X						
				X		X	X							X				

We'd love to hear your comments, questions, suggestions and adventure stories. If you know about a location that isn't in the book but should be, please let us know. We love to speak to groups and we'd be happy to talk to you about scheduling a visit. Please contact us for more information.

Facebook: Adventures Around Cincinnati
Twitter: AdventureCincy
Email: ContactUs@AdventuresAroundCincinnati.com

Enjoy your Adventures!

ABOUT THE AUTHORS

 Laura Hoevener married her husband, John, in 1994. Together they have three children, Daniel (Age 11), Anna (Age 8), and Morgan (Age 2). Laura moved to the Cincinnati area in 1999 after living in Michigan, Indiana and Wisconsin, and now lives in Miami Township in Clermont County. She has an engineering degree from the University of Wisconsin and has worked in the manufacturing and utilities industries. She is currently a professional mom who homeschools her kids and is active in her church. She has as much fun finding new things to do and exploring the area as her kids do, and she's always on the lookout for new and interesting adventures.

 Terri Weeks is a mom to Connor (age 13), Corinne (age 11), and Camille (age 8) and has been married to her husband, Curtis, for 18 years. Terri is a graduate of Purdue University and worked as a mechanical engineer prior to staying home with her kids. She now teaches part-time. Originally from Pittsburgh, she has lived in the Cincinnati area a total of 15 years, currently in Miami Township in Clermont County. She loves to travel and explore new places with her kids, both locally and afar, and thinks it's one of the best parts of parenting. Terri is active in her church, where she started and leads a group called Thriving Moms. She has a passion for encouraging moms.